The Moroccan Cookbook

The Moroccan Cookbook

By Irene F. Day

A PERIGEE BOOK

Perigee Books
are published by
G. P. Putnam's Sons
200 Madison Avenue
New York, New York 10016

Library of Congress Catalog Card Number: 77-088752
ISBN 0-399-50704-3

Cover and interior illustrations by Jeffrey Schrier
Cover design by Iris Weinstein

First Perigee printing, 1982
Printed in the United States of America

Contents

reverberated through the afternoon. In Morocco, women's fun is home-made.

Asusha, like other conservative townswomen, still wears the white draped *haik* or the tailored *djellabah* (street-length tunic with cowl) over *sarawel* (long bloomered pants), two or more skirts – or sometimes over western dress. In the south, women's *haiks* may be vivid red, sunny yellow, blue or green, often draped to reveal only one eye. The *djellabah* is practical and a leveller – it hides both wealth and rags and lends anonymity. Above the veil (*litam*) only a woman's eyes show – large, dark, luminous and enhanced with kohl. While the veil is designed to suppress temptation, such eyes can say all that is necessary. At home the Moroccan lady wears a satin kaftan, and her daughters, if exposed to a Western education, don blue jeans. The older conservative women wear headdress even indoors. One could liken it to the wimple.

The country Berber woman, on the other hand, often goes about freely and unveiled. In tribes like the Shelha she has legal rights, is the only wife, and inheritance may pass through her. Still, it is she who does the work in the fields. At Jiujiuka, an unwalled northern Riff mountain village of two hundred thatched adobes, women of the Hellzariff tribe insisted I try on their much-prized jewellery and wedding gowns in a dark windowless hut. Good humour rippled through their conversation in Berber Shelha, and they asked me questions translated through Spanish. America? They had heard of it, of course – it was somewhere in Europe. They then offered to build me a house. 'And,' they promised, 'you can come to the fields with us, and hoe corn and chop wood and grind wheat!' They approved of the effect of their traditional dress on the *Merekaneea*, and to amuse them I executed a few steps of their dance. This was met with shrieks of delight and for all I knew, I was being initiated into the tribe. But this was really *too* far removed from Pittsburgh, USA, and I took off the dress.

Their men spend their days playing the *ginbri* (a two-string guitar), fiddle and drums, for these are a tribe of musicians. They have a unique dance which they perform at the feast of Bu Jlud. The man elected Pan for that year drapes himself in a goatskin, and while drums roll and flutes trill he dances himself into a state of ecstasy. The women flee from him, shrieking, for the stick he brandishes as he loses himself in dancing bestows fertility for the coming year on whatever it strikes – wheat, women and cattle.

These men are excellent cooks and, by preference, prepare their own meals. Of course, they are also the decision-makers; their councils establish rules and dispense justice. Transgressors among them are fined in sugar, tea, smoking materials . . . to be shared among the others. A truly heavy fine such as a sheep or goat calls for a feast, which has the effect of banishing ill will and hastening forgiveness.

I was a silent participant at one of these councils. It lasted two days. We sat on rush matting on the floor of a loft, their special meeting room. Two tiny windows and an open door supplied the only ventilation while the acrid intoxicating smoke of fifty *kif* (hashish) pipes caused a thirst which drove me to drink – tea. There was plenty; glass after glass of the hot sweet mint brew was passed around. The men smiled, talked, laughed, discussed, smoked *kif* and drank tea. Once agreement was reached by vote, all applauded. There was no chief, only a chairman who acknowledged each speaker. The weight of a member's vote depends on his occupation; a quarter vote for a *ginbri*-player, a three-quarters vote for a fiddler, a half-vote for flautists; drummers and dancers don't count beyond the opinion stage. After three hours we recessed. A boy brought a brass bowl and we each held out our hands as he poured hot water over them from a kettle, and passed a towel. Then appeared a huge platter filled with tender young chickens, golden with saffron and olive oil and garnished with green olives and red peppers. One man had quietly prepared it over charcoal at the far end of the room. Someone said grace, '*Bismillah*' ('In the name of God'). We ate, as is the custom, from the common dish, dipping pieces of coarse brownish bread into the sauce and extracting with it pieces of meat, using the thumb and first two fingers of our right hands only. Next came tender young lamb cooked in oil with mint and cumin seed, and garnished with sweetened quince.

I went outside for air. Five bearded goats stalked the branches of the argan tree in front of me. In that tree, I was told, lives a very old spirit. And all around the countryside are other *djinn* (or *djnoon*) – devils which cause pain and accidents. As everyone knows, these devils often live in rocks and trees. Who is to say no? '*Allah yatak na min eldjnoon*' ('God deliver us from the evil spirits'). Something familiar caught my attention – a group of stones arranged like a tiny Stonehenge. Possibly it really was connected, for the Celts, who went to England, came here too, and the council room I had just left was framed in stone, Celt-fashion.

Someone inside began softly to tap out a rhythm on a drum with his fingertips. A flute, then a violin, joined in. Hands clapped in tempo and the men's voices picked up the tune (a ditty called 'I'll take you to a European bed, Sweetie'). One middle-aged man, urged by the others, danced. Then back to the discussions. Food was served again near midnight, a vegetable dish saturated with olive oil and topped by poached eggs. More talk, more music, then one by one they quietly left, fumbling outside in the dark for their *baboushas* (heel-less sheepskin shoes).

They left me the council room to sleep in, fully dressed – the custom here. I awoke suddenly in the morning; water still rippled in a basin which had just been set down near me. A man in a corner was praying. Several others arrived and we breakfasted on hot gruel, after which one of them – doubtless remembering the tie created by those who break bread together – solemnly announced: 'A friend of one of us is a friend of all of us. We will do anything for you. We will even kill for you.' And he meant it.

In contrast to the country village, a town (*medina*) is usually walled and includes the *kasbah* (citadel or fortified place with crenellated walls), mosques, the *souk* (market) and homes. The exteriors of homes are nondescript except for a brass door-knocker shaped in the form of the hand of Fatima, to ward off the evil eye; though houses are sometimes washed white, blue or ochre. Simplicity and anonymity are the aims; what is not seen arouses no envy. Windows seldom face the street, for the sake of security. One must enter to determine whether a house is a palace or a hovel. Inside, rooms run its length and breadth with doors and windows opening onto a central courtyard. Open to the sky, the courtyard may be graced by a small fountain or an orange tree, and possibly a well. The basic architectural design is 5,000 years old, dating from Sumerian times and still used in Spain. The rooms themselves are sparingly furnished with rugs. In more modest dwellings the *haitae* (a colourful patterned cloth) decorates the wall up to eye level. In palaces wall decoration takes the form of richly-coloured inlaid mosaic tile. Designs are always geometric, since Islam discourages portrayal of humans or animals.

Lining the walls are low couches or mattresses which serve as divans by day and beds by night.

Cooking can be done in any room over a small clay pot (*musjh-mal*) fuelled with charcoal. It is a veritable portable kitchen. Other equipment includes an earthenware pot for *tajine* (stew), mortar and pestle for mashing, a sharp knife for chopping, and skewers for barbecueing. Building a fire is time-consuming. One way is to dip a rolled-up strip of cloth in oil, imbed it in the charcoal, light it and fan madly. A quicker way is to borrow a few red hot embers from a neighbour.

In contrast to simple homes, the magnificence of the palaces at Fez and Rabat and Marrakech makes one realize that the Arabian Nights were no myth. Elaborately built, these too are uncluttered. I was once invited with a group of journalists to the Dar Batha Palace at Fez for a *diffa* – banquet. Fountains played in the courtyards; dahlia-sized zinnias were arranged in the pools; sub-tropical vegetation, hibiscus and oleander filled the wall-sur-rounded gardens where tiny gazelle gambolled. Moulded stucco fretwork ornamented the walls and the doorways shaped in the keyhole arch. We were ushered into a large traditional Moroccan reception room and seated round the walls on luxurious divans. Dusky barefoot servants brought silver ewers and basins for washing. Huge brass and copper trays were placed at intervals on stands before us.

The first course was *bastela*, pride of the Moroccan kitchen and best in Fez. It is a two-foot-wide pie of feather-light crust dusted with cinnamon and sugar. The dilemma over which piece of silverware to use was replaced by confusion over which hand to use. The foreigners, hesitant at first, soon followed their host's example, dipping in with their right hands to extract succulent morsels of pigeon prepared with parsley and onion sauce. Next came whole chickens cooked in butter with ginger and saffron, olives and onion. The lady from the London *Economist* was somewhat appalled, but between us we reduced a chicken to edible portions, each pulling with her right hand. This was followed by chickens stuffed with ground almonds, then *couscous* with lamb and onion-raisin dressing. Dessert consisted of *braewat* (very sweet cakes) and fruit. Barely able to rise, we adjourned to a high-beamed reception room furnished with European antiques and crystal chandeliers. White-garbed and turbanned servants seated cross-legged on rich carpets, presided over a Victorian silver tea service. With mint tea we were served biscuits and Gazelles' Horns (a delicious light pastry made of crushed almonds). Music accompanies every event in Morocco, and here an Andalusian orchestra alternated with a European one. After three glasses of mint tea – which a guest may not refuse – we took our leave, for this is the host's signal that the banquet has ended.

A *diffa* in a tent is something else – a sort of glorified picnic in the countryside. Inside a mighty tent seating one hundred or more people, rugs are spread over the ground. Brass tables are surrounded by hassocks or stools to seat seven or eight people. The food is carried to the tent in the *tbeqa* (a round metal or wicker container with a high conical cover) to keep the heat in and the flies out. A simple menu might consist of: *mischui* (whole roast lamb), chickens boiled in oil and spices with prunes, roast chickens, followed by lamb, then *couscous* with a sweet dressing, and fruit. And, of course, tea. After the post-prandial wash-up, an attendant sprinkles you with essence of orange blossom or rose petals to dispel food odours.

Whether for a *diffa* or a simple home meal, it is the man who generally does the shopping. Women stay indoors. He makes the daily excursion into the open-air *souks* where everything, fresh bread and heaping mounds of red, green, yellow vegetables, spices and meats lies exposed to the air. Even clothing, jewellery and transistor radios are on sale there. Cold storage is rare, but foods are bought fresh daily by choice. The shopping trip provides social life, for at the *souk* the shopper meets his friends, lingers to gossip or play a game of *dama* (chess), or talks politics in the coffee houses – over tea. It is interesting to watch two men greet each other; they may embrace, each throwing a kissing motion over the left shoulder of the other. With you or me, if he knows us, he will shake hands, then place his hand briefly over his heart. He usually breakfasts in the market, for the charcoal fires are not yet started at home. He may have *sfinge* (a doughnut), or *ulk'tiban* (bits of meat) skewered and roasted, or steaming hot *hareera* (a cream soup), the traditional Ramadan breakfast, set out on a counter in blue and orange bowls.

The *souk* is the hub of most Moroccan activity. From early morning when the *muezzin* cries out his first summons to prayer (now electronically amplified) from the minaret: '*La Ilaha il-la*

Allah' ('There is no god but God'), until the last call at night, a Moroccan town is distinguishable by its sounds, sights and aromas, most of them emanating from the *souk*.

By dawn Berber country women wearing broad straw hats and red, white and black striped skirts are plodding to market with loads of vegetables or fruit on their backs, chattering and calling among themselves. If there is a donkey, it will be a man who rides him. Women walk. The donkey's hoofs striking the cobblestones beat out a 'ticketa-tocketa' as he carries panniers of vegetables, grain, wood or charcoal to market. His owner warns pedestrians out of the way by shouting, *'Balek! balek!'* The cry of fish peddler mingles with the tinkle of the waterseller's bell. A sheep changes hands, bleating a protest. The raucous bray of the ass (christened the 'Moroccan nightingale' by one European), rises above the radio blast of music made in Cairo. At noon, the cacophonous ringing and clanging of mortar and pestle in a hundred kitchens announces lunch. Afternoon brings a lull; some seek the shade of a truck or tree to sleep. The Berber women, still in high good humour, march out of town barefoot, carrying their slippers and a supply of sugar or flour or tea. The aroma of fresh bread pervades the air. In the gathering shadows, the day's events are discussed. Whatever has happened or been said a few hours earlier has now come full circle . . . elaborately embellished; this is known as the *souk* telegraph.

Morocco's *souks* are the most fascinating and colourful, anywhere, not excepting those at Cairo, Damascus or Istanbul, and they are cleaner. One of the best is at Fez, also noted for its university, the refinement of its people, its cuisine, and its gold, silver, wood and leather work. Another good *souk* is at Meknes in the heart of rich agricultural land. Here you might see a blue-gowned black 'doctor' from the south, barefoot, but sporting an enormous gold wristwatch, with his 'medications' – ground lizard, herbs and potions – spread out on the ground. His clients want to be rid of a rival, to make a successful conquest, or just generally to enjoy greater sexual prowess. By the gate sits a public scribe, ready, for a few dirhams, to read or write letters for his unschooled countrymen.

The most exciting *souk* of all is in Marrakech, the 900-year-old southern city which is a red and green oasis lying at the foot of the Greater Atlas Mountains. Its irrigated gardens, the Aguedal, overflow with purple bougainvillea, jacaranda, pomegranate and orange groves. Miles of ancient crenellated red mud wall lace the green gardens. And although only mule carts were meant to pass through their arched gateways, the driver of a bus in which I rode wedged through with a crunch. A bit of old rampart crumbled in a cloud of dust, the fenders bent slightly. The next gateway, to the rising amusement of the passengers, also had to be negotiated and somewhat altered. Of what importance, after all, are a bit of fender and a bit of wall? This is Africa – everything gives a little.

Marrakech was once a caravan station serving the slave route from Timbuktu, and here, deeper in Africa, the people range in hue from white to beige to charcoal black. Islam, and Morocco, recognize no colour barriers, and the occasional blue-eyed person may be descended from one of the 25,000 Christian slaves once known to be held in the country.

Narrow lanes bordered by stalls form a labyrinth of passages where the sun shafting the overhead lattice splashes patterns on the pathways of the *souk* and *medina*. Hurly-burly activity reigns from morning until night, with a cacophony of voices raised in animated bargaining. The animation arises from recognition on both sides that one never pays the first price asked . . . to do so is to rob the transaction of its fun.

In the artisans' quarters, men bend over their embroidering, leather bags or looms. Small boys with queues (*'ugun*) hold skeins of wool as they begin long years of apprenticeship. Silver is worked into poniards or bracelets and geometric designs are etched onto brass or copper or silver trays. A young man sits in a cubbyhole open to the street; he holds a chisel in one hand while revolving a stick of wood with his foot; in less than a minute the stick has become a turned table leg. The wool dyers' quarters present a kaleidoscope of colour; wet skeins hung to dry high over the streets splash the air with reds and oranges, blues and yellows.

In Plaza Djemaa el-Fna bearded holy men tell stories each evening to circles of listeners. Men and boys sit on the ground around him, their handsome features thrown into relief by the flickering light from a kerosene lantern. Now and then the narrator bangs on a *darbooka* (tambourine) to punctuate his phrases and attract more audience. When he stops speaking, without ending the story so that his listeners will return the next evening, the tambourine is passed for a collection. Such tales, often about Noah or Jonah or

Sinbad, arrived from the Chaldean via the Hebrew, thence into Latin and Arabic. One can visualize other tribesmen, further East, gathered about their tents at night 2,000 years ago, listening to just such a teller of tales.

While under the surface Moroccans continue to harbour the superstitions of their forebears, to worship spirits and local saints, both living and dead, and to practice witchcraft, the nominal and recognized religion is Islam, with which the Arabs proselytized them. A good Moslem prays five times a day no matter where he finds himself. You may see him at noon crossing a field by donkey; he stops abruptly, alights and kneels on the ground, bowing his head low towards the East. Women need not do so – their different place in the scheme of things is accepted by both sexes – there is no Women's Lib movement here, as yet. Though faceless to the outside world, they exert strong influence in home and family. They may not enter the mosques except for one night of the year, and non-Moslems – never. Friday is the Holy Day, and the day to go to the *hamman* (public bath). Moroccans are fastidious, even though they know little about germs or the danger represented by the ubiquitous flies. (A friend of mine was delighted by the way her *fatima* kept the house spotless, washing floors daily, until she discovered to her consternation that the woman used the same cloth to wash the inside of the frigidaire.)

In the interests of cleanliness and of religion, the Moroccan man's head is usually shaven; Mohammed declared that whoever left a hair of his body unwashed before prayers could not enter heaven; it would be a nuisance to wash every hair five times a day, even though washing is often ritual. Moslem men always wear a turban or *tarboush* or *chechia* (fez) in public. The Prophet reasoned that if no legal injunction forced his followers to wear head covering, many would die of sunstroke. (Koranic law is *the* law in Moslem countries.) His other dress consists of the *djellabah*, if he still wears one, over Western or Eastern clothes. In the country he might add a burnoose (*silham*) of woven brown goat hair or fine white wool – to keep him cool in summer and warm in winter.

A vital religious act in Islamic countries is the observance of Ramadan. Believers must deny themselves food, drink, smoking and sexual relations between sunrise and sunset. The month-long fast is a period of atonement and forgiveness, and only the very young, the very old, the feeble, the pregnant and the traveller are exempt. Fasting begins the day after the new moon of Ramadan has been sighted and announced by the thunder of cannon or a roll of drums. Each day's fasting ends when the sun sets. Breakfast is ready and waiting. Then come visits with friends and neighbours. Around midnight the plaintive notes of the *gaita* – a reed instrument sounding like a bagpipe – played from atop the minaret announces time for dinner. Later, the pulsating beat of scores of drums reverberates across the dark hills, swelling and drifting away as the breeze rises and falls. There will be dancing by the men – and by the women if they are alone. Those who work Western hours usually go to bed after this midnight 'lunch', but those who stay up until the *gaita* wails again will have supper just before dawn.

The twenty-sixth day of Ramadan, called *Lailat Kadal*, commemorates Mohammed's receiving from God the dicta he wrote in the Koran. Candles and incense burn all night in the mosques so that the faithful may spend the night in prayer. According to the country people, all devils are tied up for this occasion.

The last day of Ramadan is *Eid el-Fitra* (The Feast of the Alms). Beginning about 3.00 a.m., the poor come to claim charity. The head of each household must give each caller a *luni* (a measure) of grain, flour or money. The measure must be four double handfuls 'with the hands held neither completely open nor tightly shut'. Ragged alms-gatherers, carrying sacks, rush through the streets banging on one door after another, to complete their rounds before dawn.

Two months after Ramadan on *Eid el-Kebir* (The Big Feast), everyone who can, sacrifices a sheep in commemoration of Abraham's sacrifice. Tradition decrees the meat be shared with those who cannot afford the money for such expenditure.

Ever since the days of Abraham, when wandering tribes needed to reinforce their labour supply by increasing, procreation has been a paramount concern. What man is a man who has no sons? In holding up his child to be admired the Moroccan is privately vindicating his own virility, especially if the offspring is male. The more boys he can sire, the better; interdependence is built in. It is a social disgrace not to bring children into the world – and failure to do so is common ground for divorce. And, if one cannot support them, well, then there is a saying, 'I love my child well enough to abandon him.' With luck, the child will find a better chance in life with someone else. Children are freely, without legal formalities, adopted into other families. Such waifs, unfortunately, are often made servants; yet they are part of a family. They eat, and they have a home.

Food, religion and sex are the principal ingredients of Moroccan life. A man gets a wife through intermediaries. He may have seen her on the street or his brother's wife may suggest a likely maiden. Traditionally, the first time husband and wife meet alone is in bed. There is no religious ceremony. A contract is drawn up before the *hadul*, the government's representative, and signed. Then the celebrations begin, the bride's and the groom's separately.

Music from tambourine, drums, *ginbri* had already been playing for the better part of three days and nights when I was accorded the unusual privilege of witnessing a bridegroom's celebration. I climbed a ladder to a flat roof. A voice in the dark said *'Le bas'* ('Hello!') and a small loaf of bread was thrust into my hands; this symbolic gift is made to each guest to assure fertility (whether the newlyweds' or one's own I never found out, but I took no chances by eating it). A glass of hot tea arrived, then another and another – 'against the cold'.

In the patio below, a rich red Oriental carpet covered the floor. Barefoot men, chatting, smoking, and drinking tea (no alcohol is served here), lounged on low divans; seated in their midst was the groom, king of the day. Three musicians played and hands clapped accompaniment; a young man sang a monotonous, nasal tune; another gyrated in their midst, balancing a glass of water on his head. The tempo increased, someone called: *'Aaaiy-WAH!'* (roughly translated, 'Yeah, Man!' whereas a simple *aywah* means 'yes'). The women around me pierced the night with the shrill *zara'eet* – cry of approval, best described as 'eul-eul-eul-eul'. The men never looked up. Later, the hat would be passed; Moroccans spend what they have today and it is usually feast or famine – tomorrow will see another's turn to contribute. Food was served to the men; anything left over would be later handed up to the women.

'Safi', ('enough'), I decided, and backed down the ladder to go and see the bride. Having left her own party she now arrived in the courtyard of her husband's home, tucked into a curtained box (*ambarya*) aboard a mule. Women attendants carried her to bed, for her feet must not touch the ground. I caught only a glimpse of

her. Hands and hair were heavily hennaed, strands of gold beads cascaded over her ample bosom, a dozen bracelets ringed her sleeved arms. Blue tattoos on her chin and forehead formed small five-pronged designs. One must thwart the evil eye by tattooing baby girls – who as today's adults spend a fortune trying to eradicate the marks. The bride is sombre to demonstrate her new dignity – but she is probably frightened. She will meet the groom later in the morning. If he doesn't like her or she proves not to be a virgin, he can send her packing home to *Ayma* (Mama). Usually she stays, however, whatever the case – pride inhibits public acknowledgement of having made a poor bargain.

It was 4.00 a.m., and now we were drawn down a narrow lane by the more rhythmic, more exciting, more African tympany of drums and woodwinds. A gate and door stood open. Men and women dressed in knee-length white gowns clapped in unison; negro musicians played as a woman and a man danced, singly, frenziedly, slapping their legs with heavy knives which left cross-hatches of blood. The woman fell unconscious to the floor and the music stopped abruptly. 'Don't go near,' cautioned a friend. 'In this state they don't know what they do.' These dancers were members of the Djelaelli sect, who are said to eat scorpions and serpents as proof of their devotion to God.

The casual observer might never encounter such a scene. He sees old quarters and city skyscrapers dazzling white in the sun, endures the begging of shoeshine boys; he notes the differences in dress and customs, and might partake in a *diffa* or watch the powder play when bands of brightly-dressed horsemen charge each other, firing rifles; he invariably absorbs some of the drama and senses something of the magic which remains in Morocco in spite of all the changes.

These changes are inevitable and some are for the good. More young people are getting an education beyond chanting and memorizing the Koran. The French during their 1912–56 occupation built roads and suppressed banditry; one can now drive safely between cities where fifty years ago a caravan had to be organized. Awareness of the outside world is increasing among educated Moroccans. Some young women are dropping the veil, and the idea of romantic love is taking hold. There is growing emulation of the West, on the surface.

But out across the *bled* (plains), up in the *sjebal* (hills), down in the desert, traditions endure – integral and vital to the way of life. *Inshallah* – God willing – the good things of that life, the dignified pace, the simplicity, the colour, the naturalness, will remain in spite of the new layer of modernity. When the differences between one people and another disappear, when traditions are submerged and snuffed out, when we have all 'progressed' to the point where everyone of us lives and thinks and cooks alike, then the fun, the spice of life too, will be gone. The spice of life in Morocco spills over into the cuisine. It is often said that to know a country and its people one must know its food; and the food of Morocco still teaches one about a country rich in individuality and charm.

NOTES

About quantities. This is not the kind of cooking which always demands accuracy. Where I have not given exact measurements you can take it that your own judgement or taste should be the guide, as it would be for a Moroccan cook.

To those cooks who are lucky enough to find it; the '*true*' saffron is a dark, thin, red thread, available in Spain and North Africa; and the veriest pinch – say, $\frac{1}{4}$ to $\frac{1}{2}$ inch long – suffices.

Garlic: use less than the recipes suggest if you dislike it, but it would be a pity to omit it. In this kind of well-seasoned cooking the taste blends in, adding to the general deliciousness without obtruding.

THE CLASSIC
SEVEN

COUSCOUS

(*Suksoo* or *Kesksu*; Berber: '*Ta'am*')

Couscous is by way of being the national dish and the standby of rich and poor alike. It is to North Africa what spaghetti is to Italy, rice to China, beans to Brazil. Deriving from semolina and flour, it appears on the table as a great white heap of fine pellet-like grains. The heap is shaped like a volcano, with lamb, mutton or chicken layed in the crater on top, and all dressed either with a vegetable garnish, or with a sweet or hot sauce and almonds.

Couscous is the classic Friday (Islamic Sabbath) dish, as well as the central item at marriage feasts and fete days. On the third day of Aid-el-Kebir, the Fete of the Lamb, the head of the animal provides the meat content. Originally called 'Suksoo' in local dialect, it came out 'Couscous' when pronounced by French colonists, and so it has become known among North Africans themselves. Many European restaurants feature it, and it makes a substantial meal on any occasion.

The visitor's introduction to couscous comes almost as soon as he arrives in the country. Since Arabs usually eat without the aid of silverware, using the thumb and first two fingers of the right hand only, the small grains present a real challenge. A fistful is first worked into a ball, then carried to the mouth – slowly. Those of us with less skill are given a large spoon for eating this dish, and some 'Europeanized' families make this concession to Western efficiency in their own homes. The meat morsels are picked out with the right hand, and it is customary when a guest is present, for the host to select the choicest bits in any dish and personally feed them to his guest.

In all frankness, Westerners prefer the garnish and meat to the semolina, (the couscous itself) since the semolina is very heavy.

Like noodles or spaghetti and other grain derivatives the semolina part of the couscous requires advance preparation. This basic ingredient is however now available, already prepared and packaged, at the *bakkal* (grocery), and I myself prefer making the short trip to the *bakkal* to spending hours in the kitchen. (Moroccans who have returned from the U.S. tell me they were able to buy the packaged product, made at Casablanca, under the brand name of 'Baruck', from Saad Ben Mohammed, 317 W. 43rd Street, New York City.)

For the edification of more ambitious cooks, however, I describe here the way the vast majority of Moroccan women still prepare couscous.

Half the following recipe will serve six; the other half may be kept dry in a tin for future use.

The Base

STEP 1 Place 3 cups of semolina in a ring in a large wide bowl or basin. Leave the centre area inside the circle of the semolina ring free. Now, with a spoon, flick a little water into the centre, and in quick, light motions, scoop the semolina over the centre.

Sprinkle over the grains 3 tablespoons salt and 1 tablespoon flour, and mix lightly and quickly in a clockwise motion with the flats of the hands. This process gradually forms the meal into tiny grain-like bits about buckshot – or fine, uncooked tapioca size.

When some grains have formed, sift out the semolina in a large, medium-meshed, wire sieve. The fine grains which remain in the sieve are the couscous. The big globs on top and the loose grain which has fallen through are to be returned to the mixing bowl and reworked in the same manner, using a sprinkling of water and 1 tablespoon of flour to lend cohesion.

In all you will use 1lb of semolina to *not more than* ½ lb flour.

STEP 2 Steam the fine finished grains in a colander over boiling water.

STEP 3 Place grains, spread out on a board or cloth in a dry, airy place. When dry the next day, couscous may be prepared for eating – or may be kept in an airtight container for future use.

An English friend married to a Moroccan was specific in giving me the directions she had learned from her mother-in-law. The first time, she says, may take up to three hours, but a practiced couscous cook can get it down to one hour.

Preparing Couscous for Eating

When preparing couscous for the table, begin first to cook the meat and garnish. Three-quarters of an hour before it is done and ready to serve, proceed with couscous preparation.

STEP 1 Put 4 cups of dried couscous grains in a large wide bowl or basin. Wash quickly and lightly with 2–3 cups of cool water; then immediately drain off water. Allow the wet grains to sit untouched for 15 minutes, during which time they will swell up. Then work them around lightly through the fingers to loosen and separate them.

STEP 2 Turn *half* the couscous into a coarse strainer or sieve and let it steam over boiling water or over the casserole of cooking meat. If steam escapes at sides of pan, seal the pot and colander with a wet cloth or a flour-water paste. .When steam has begun to pass quite well through the couscous, add the balance of unsteamed grains in on top. Vapour should pass through this too. Steam a half hour in all. Grains should be soft, but firm and not mushy. If still hard, when removed, sprinkle with $\frac{1}{4}$ to $\frac{1}{2}$ cup of cold water which has been salted, pass the hands through the grains to separate them and return to steam again.

STEP 3 Once couscous has been steamed, empty it out into the wide basin and by hand mix in, separating the grains:
2 tablespoons butter
$\frac{1}{2}$ cup meat stock (to slightly moisten)
$\frac{1}{2}$ teaspoon black pepper
1 teaspoon cinnamon (optional)

The Face of the Couscous (1)
The Tetuan Method

Fatima, who is by now happily making dinner guests at the Moroccan Embassy in Washington sing praises of her country's food, makes the best couscous I have ever tasted. The garnish of meat and onions she calls in her original way, 'the face of the couscous'. Here is how she prepared the all-important garnish in the Benabud home in Tetuan.

The Meat Content

Place in a deep casserole:

> 4½–5 lb leg of lamb (first crack bones)

Lay in over the meat, one by one:

> ¼ cup onion, cut up
> 1 tablespoon salt
> 1 teaspoon black pepper
> ½ teaspoon powdered saffron
> ¾ cup olive oil

Cover and cook over a high fire for 3 minutes, then add:

> ½ cup butter (or margarine)

Continue cooking, mixing ingredients around almost constantly. After 15 minutes, when oil and spices are almost absorbed by the meat, add:

> 2 quarts boiling hot water
> ¾ cup chick-peas (which have soaked overnight)

At the end of an hour's cooking time – and when chick-peas are cooked, the meat should be done.

The Dressing

While the meat cooks, proceed with preparation of the dressing. Put together in a small saucepan:

> 3 cups onion, sliced fine *lengthwise*
> ½ teaspoon cinnamon
> ½ teaspoon black pepper
> ½ teaspoon powdered saffron
> ¼ cup butter
> 1 teaspoon salt

Wilt the above over a medium-slow fire, making sure the lid of the pan is on tight. Check and stir frequently. After 20 minutes – or when the onion is golden and well cooked, add:

> 1 cup meat stock

Continue cooking for 15 minutes more. Then add:

> ½ cup raisins (which have soaked ½ hour in water)

Continue cooking 10 minutes more, stirring occasionally.

SERVE   In the Moroccan style, heap the semolina in a mound on a large round serving platter; make a depression in the top. Place the meat (without broth) in the depression. The chick-peas from the meat broth have been added into the onion-raisin dressing; garnish the top with this. The same procedure may be followed when serving on individual plates, using 2 cupfuls of semolina to a serving.

Two sauces are put on the table: (1) a bowl of the meat broth, and (2) hot sauce to be found further on in couscous recipes.

Important Beverages should not accompany couscous – it has a way of expanding – and a half–hour margin on both sides should be allowed before or after drinking anything. Mint tea a half hour after eating is especially recommended.

Couscous (2)
Tangerine Style

The Meat

Put together in casserole:

    2½ lbs stewing meat, cut in 1½" cubes
    ½ cup parsley, chopped fine
    1½ cups onion, cubed coarsely
    1 teaspoon black pepper
    ¼ teaspoon ginger
    ¼ teaspoon nutmeg
    ¼ teaspoon curry
    ¼ teaspoon saffron
    1 teaspoon cinnamon
    2 tablespoons salt
    ½ cup olive oil
    1 tablespoon butter

Cover and cook over medium-high fire for 15 minutes, stirring frequently. Then add:

    5 cups hot water

Recover and continue cooking.

Ten minutes before meat will be done, add:

    1½ cups seedless raisins (which have soaked ½ hour in water)

The Dressing

Boil together until tender:

    1 cup seedless raisins
    1½ cups onion, sliced fine lengthwise

$\frac{1}{2}$ teaspoon saffron
1 dessertspoon salt butter
1 dessertspoon cinnamon
6 tablespoons meat stock

SERVE   As in Couscous (1), first heaping the steamed couscous in a mound on a serving platter, then the meat without stock on top, with dressing over that. Dampen whole dish a little with meat stock.

Couscous (3)
Algerian Couscous

The meat content of this dish which is frequently prepared in Morocco may be chicken, veal, beef, goat, lamb or mutton, but chicken and the traditional lamb lend best flavours. The base of the couscous, the semolina, is always prepared in the same way. See Preparing Couscous for Eating, Step 1.

Meat and Vegetable Garnish

STEP 1   Put together in large casserole:
 $1\frac{1}{2}$ lbs meat, cut in $1\frac{1}{2}$" cubes
 $\frac{1}{2}$ cup parsley, chopped fine
 1 cup onion, cubed coarsely
 1 teaspoon black pepper
 $\frac{1}{2}$ teaspoon saffron
 1 tablespoon cinnamon
 2 scant tablespoons salt
 1 cup olive oil
 1 tablespoon butter
 a cracked bone or two to give added flavour
Cook the above together over a medium–high fire for 15 minutes, stirring frequently. Then add:
 5 cups hot water
Continue cooking until meat is tender and nearly done (about $1\frac{1}{2}$ hours, depending on quality).

STEP 2   When meat is about done, add in:
 6–8 carrots, each sliced lengthwise
 6–8 turnips, ,,   ,,   ,,
Meat and vegetables are ready when carrots are cooked.

STEP 3 Apart, boil in salted water until cooked:

1–2 cups chick-peas (which have soaked overnight)

STEP 4 Apart, also boil in *unsalted* water for about 10 minutes or until tender:

1 cup seedless raisins

TO SERVE Atop the mound of couscous place the meat, which has been removed from its broth. Decorate the top and sides with carrots and turnips; toss over all the chick-peas and raisins (drained). Dress with a bit of meat sauce.

Variations Instead of chick-peas, or in addition to them, 2 cups of almonds may be used. For couscous they should be blanched and the skins rubbed off. Then they should boil in water with a pinch of bicarbonate of soda for 20 minutes or until nearly soft. Once drained and dry, they are lightly toasted in butter.

Hot Sauce for Couscous

A little sauce is important to couscous with meat and vegetables. This may consist simply of the meat broth, but for those who like it 'hot', a separate cup of hot sauce is set on the table. It should be used with discretion, for a little goes a long way. Personally, I like a drop or two on the semolina grains in all but the sweet couscous dishes, finding them just a bit bland without it. To make the hot sauce:

Boil together for a couple of minutes:

1 cup meat broth

½ teaspoon hot red peppers

To this when done may be added:

4 tablespoons blanched, toasted almonds, chopped up (optional)

Chicken with Couscous or Vermicelli (4)
Midfoon

STEP 1 Cook the chicken, using the same procedure as in bastela, Step 1. Remove meat from sauce and bone.

STEP 2 Steam couscous for ½ hour in colander over boiling water. Remove and mix in 1 tablespoon butter.

SERVE Place on platter a layer of couscous about 1½" thick; then a layer of the meat filling, then another layer of couscous. Sprinkle sugar and cinnamon over all.

Couscous Porridge (5)

Couscous is steamed for $\frac{1}{2}$ hour in colander over boiling water, then 2 or more tablespoons of butter are mixed into it. This may be eaten like a porridge by adding milk, and sprinkled with cinnamon and sugar.

Couscous with Buttermilk (6)
Sikuk

Couscous is steamed for $\frac{1}{2}$ hour in colander over boiling water, then combined with buttermilk and eaten with or without sugar.

Couscous (7)
Marrakech Style

Moroccans like sweet dishes sweet. This sweet couscous – served usually as a final course before fruits and *braewats*, is surprisingly good and based on onions and raisins. Some cooks may react to the first reading of the recipe the way Europeans react to the American ham with pineapple or sweet potatoes with marshmallows. But the Americans like them, and so do some Europeans after they have tasted them. The sauce here should be abundant, and balanced in the eating with the blander couscous.

STEP I Steam or wilt together:

    4 cups sweet white onions, sliced fine lengthwise
    2 tablespoons cinnamon
    $\frac{1}{2}$ teaspoon powdered saffron
    $\frac{1}{2}$ cup butter
    $\frac{1}{2}$ teaspoon salt
    I teaspoon ginger

Cover and cook over low fire, stirring frequently.

When onion is golden (about 20 minutes), add in:

> 1½ cups water (or meat broth)
> 1 cup sugar
> 2 cups seedless raisins (which have soaked several hours in water)

Cover and continue cooking over a slow fire, stirring frequently, for 25–30 minutes more. When finished, sauce should be well blended, rather thick, with almost no liquid.

SERVE Hot, over the basic standard couscous. In dressing the heap of couscous grains, it is prettiest and neatest when it fills only the top of the crater.

Couscous with Quince Garnish (8)

Follow basic couscous preparation (Style 1) with or without use of meat.

Stew together until tender, but still firm:

> 6 quinces, peeled and quartered
> 1 tablespoon cinnamon
> ½ cup sugar
> water to cover

SERVE Warm and serve as garnish over basic couscous.

MISCHUI
Whole roast lamb or sheep
꒱꒰ꗈꙶꙶꙶꙶ꒱꒰

The woolly lamb figures among a Moroccan's most prized posses-
sions. The man who lives in the mud hut is comparatively wealthy
if he owns a dozen head. Along with the goat, the sheep is at once
North Africa's curse and blessing. Hills and fields grow dry and
brown in rainless months, but these four-footed providers of meat,
milk, and cloth which have denuded the land, survive.

A lamb or sheep roasted whole in a mud oven, or barbecued
slowly over hot coals is a special treat, reserved to feast days,
marriages, saints' days. The sheep is also the animal sacrificed
by all Moroccans for the Feast of Aid-el-Kebir, which marks the
end of the annual pilgrimage to Mecca. At this time new clothes
are donned, gifts exchanged, and work put aside. The slaughter
itself commemorates the sacrifice of Abraham of his son.

One day friends took us to attend the feast in honour of Saint
Sidi Boud Ali, some twenty miles south of Larache. There we
came upon acres of open country mushrooming with canvas and
hide tents.

On such occasions where people gather from the outlying
countryside, there are horse races, powder play, music, dancing
and feasting for several days. Dotting this acreage were the brightly
decorated tents of important Caids (tribal chiefs) and their families.
Colourfully woven rugs and bright patterned cushions and divans
furnished the interiors of the tents, and rugs were laid outside on
the ground as well. Heavy brass trays served as tables. Servants –
considered members of the family – were busily preparing food.
We wended our way through the maze of tents to find a certain
Caid, a white-bearded, old patriarch of gentle mien.

'A'selema, le bas,' he greeted us. ('May no harm be with you.')

We sat on the divans set in a rectangle on the rugs. Mint tea
and almond cakes were passed while news, with no detail omitted,
was exchanged for a half hour or so.

Nearby was what appeared to be a large mound of mud about
five feet high. A servant went to it, swept some dry clay from the
top and removed a metal sheet laid across it.

'*Shnu hada?*' I asked the old man. ('What's that?')

'*Hada frra dishwa – deba chuf,*' he replied. ('That is a mischui oven.')

With some struggling, the servant lifted out a golden brown carcass spitted on a pole. The savoury aroma of roasted meat spiced the air and whetted our appetites.

'How was it done?' I wanted to know.

'*Ah, blati, blati,*' he said. ('Take it easy.') '*Kayiss umum bat sucksi.*' ('First eat, then ask.')

A servant brought around the ewer for washing hands. Then he set half the carcass on a wood slab on the table before us.

Round, flat loaves of bread were broken apart and passed. A dish of salt mixed with crushed cumin seed was set on the table.

Mischui, to be good, must be eaten while still hot, and for some time no one spoke beyond exclamations of approval. Unlike many Westerners, Easterners express their appreciation of good food. We tore chunks of meat from the carcass with our fingers (of the right hand), eating according to local custom. The rib meat, particularly on a young animal, is the best.

It was *mezienne, mezienne bizeff* – very, very good.

Just as we were finishing, leaving enough meat on the nearly demolished carcass for the servants, the Caid's son arrived with a dozen young men on horseback and the old man rose to receive them. Making them welcome, he commanded them also to be seated.

'You're in luck,' he turned to me, and added, 'Now you will see how to turn a lamb into mischui. We are going to prepare two more – each in a different manner.'

Mischui (1)

A small aperture at the foot of the mud and brick structure was removed, and a roaring fire kindled on the ground inside the oven. The fire was fed for an hour and a half, and then, all but the hot red embers removed.

A skinned and gutted sheep was spitted on a sturdy pole and lowered from above into the oven. The oven is only slightly wider than the animal so that it is placed upright with the top of the pole leaning against the inside of the oven wall. A sheet of metal was laid over the top and fresh mud over that. The 'door' at the bottom was re-sealed with bricks and fresh mud.

That sheep became mischui during the three hours it remained inside the hot oven, becoming roasted slowly and thoroughly by the heat retained there.

Mischui (2)

'*Deba azjee choof en'teena*' ('Come and see the second one'), said the Caid, once Mischui No. 1 had been cached in its mud cocoon.

Beyond his tent in an open space, a bed of glowing hot coals four feet wide by six feet in length spread over the ground. Over this, about eighteen inches above them, was spitted a young lamb, on a long rod, one end of which rested on an elevation of bricks. A man holding the other end turned it constantly by means of a handle. (The mystery of what happens to old Ford cranks and rods is now cleared up.) Another man stood by to frequently baste the meat with a mixture of butter, salt and ground cumin seed. (2 lbs butter, $\frac{1}{2}$ cup salt, $\frac{1}{4}$ cup crushed cumin seed.)

In the $2\frac{1}{2}$–3 hours it took for the animal to barbecue, it had grown dark; the perfume of roasting meat filled the air.

We gathered round on the divans, and one man began to tell a story as the others listened attentively. A few smoked. There was a quietness and peace in this reunion. Were I a Moroccan woman, I should have had to content myself by listening from behind the tent flaps with my sisters, and to partake later of whatever remained of the food. The story ended and the men applauded. Mischui (2) was set on several tables before us. Behind us, five musicians began to sing and to play on *tambour*, *ginbri* and flute.

If the oven-roasted mischui had been *mezienne bizeff*, this was doubly so, and the one most palatable to Western tastes. (Red wine, though forbidden Moslems, makes an excellent companion.)

Mischui Oven (1)

For those who live in the wide open spaces and have the time and yen to so amuse themselves, here are directions for making the oven. Lots of wet mud and stones or old broken bricks are all the construction materials needed. Moroccans slap this temporary structure together in something like half an hour.

First, draw a circle on the ground $2\frac{1}{2}$ feet in diameter. Within that circle, draw another 4 inches shorter in diameter, and hollow out the ground inside the inner circle to a depth of 10 inches.

Select a 10-inch section of the circumference as the front of the oven. Dig a path 10 inches deep and extending out about $1\frac{1}{2}$ feet from the front of the oven, as an approach.

Moisten the earth on the outer circle. Slap a layer of wet mud about 4 inches wide around the outside of the circle. Sink rocks, stones, broken or whole bricks in the mud. Leave a gap at the front where the doorway will be. Line a few inches of the approach with mud and brick. Then add onto the circle of the oven layers of mud alternately with layers of stones and bricks to build the walls. When the wall reaches a height of 10 inches, lay a bar of iron or flat rock across the door opening, completing the circle of the rising wall, and continue building until the cylinder reaches a height of 3 feet. Then start to graduate the circle inward a little by placing stones closer to the interior, shortening the diameter. Continue building the oven up till it reaches about $4\frac{1}{2}$ feet high in all – or high enough to accommodate the length of the animal. With wet mud, smooth the outside wall, covering the bricks, etc.

Build a roaring fire inside the oven. Keep feeding it, adding more fuel for $1\frac{1}{2}$ hours. The oven should be red hot inside. Then, remove whatever actual fire there is, leaving only hot red coals.

Introduce the carcass, spitted on a stout freshly cut pole or iron rod slightly longer than the animal, into the oven from above. With mud and bricks, quickly close the bottom door. Cover the open top with a sheet of metal, overlaying it with fresh mud. After 3 hours in the oven, depending on size and age of animal, it is mischui and ready to eat – immediately.

Mischui (2)

Another style of oven is frequently built, long and low to accommodate the carcass lengthwise. A shallow basin is first hollowed out of the ground, then cemented over with mud. The walls are built up in a rectangle surrounding this, using mud and brick or stones alternately, to a height of 2 feet. Leave a door at the bottom big enough to insert the carcass later. The inside walls are made smooth with mud, and the top is formed by supporting the mud and stones with sticks which may be pulled out later.

Once the oven is completed, a roaring fire is built inside and kept going for about 2 hours. Then all, including the embers are removed, and the interior thoroughly cleaned with a cloth. The meat is placed inside where the fire was, and the door sealed with mud and bricks and left for 1 to 2 hours, depending on the size of the animal. This method is also used for roasting beef.

Mischui in the Kitchen

Make mischui in the kitchen using a quarter of a lamb; ribs are best.

STEP 1 Pound into a paste in mortar:
    1 tablespoon cumin seed
    1 teaspoon saffron
    2 tablespoons salt
    $\frac{1}{2}$ teaspoon hot red pepper
    1 head garlic, peeled
    $\frac{1}{2}$ cup parsley, minced

Rub paste all over meat; put in pot or roasting pan with:
    1 lb butter

STEP 2 Cook over medium-high fire atop stove, with lid on: baste from time to time. Or roast in hot oven in open roasting pan; baste often.

HAREERA
A rich and nourishing soup

'Eat and drink until so much of the dawn appears that
a white thread may be distinguished from a black thread;
then keep the fast completely until night.' *Koran.*

One of the pillars of Islam is the strict observance of the annual
month-long Fast of Ramadan. Throughout the twenty-nine,
or thirty days of Ramadan, Moslems must deny themselves all
food and drink (and tobacco) between the hours of sunrise and
sunset. Ramadan parallels the Jewish Yom Kippur as a period of
atonement and forgiveness.

The fast is truly a test to the Faithful, and only the sick, the
pregnant, children, prisoners and those in battle or travelling
are exempt. This very important period may fall in any season
including the hottest, since Islam's twelve lunar months make 354
days; thus over the years the months move through the seasons.
Abstinence from food and drink are trying, at best, and an ordeal
for those who must work all day. Sleep is rationed, and the strain
of the fast overcomes some people. Fasting begins the day after
the new moon of Ramadan has been sighted, and the command to
begin is announced by the thunder of cannon or the roll of drums.

When the official viewer sees the last sunray disappear each
day, the cannon is fired, bringing relief like a fresh rain which
clears electrically charged air. Traditionally Moroccans break
the fast with hareera, a nutritious soup which quickly restores
waning energies, quenches thirst, soothes flaring tempers, helps
the Faithful sustain the fast.

Later at night, the tympany of drums reverberates across the
hills until well beyond midnight. In the homes there may be
dancing by the men – or by the women if they are alone – though
they never dance in couples. Two hours after soup time, the
main meal is eaten, and about this time the notes of the *gaitra*
(reed horn which sounds like bagpipe) may be heard coming from

the mosque. Supper will be eaten before the first cock crows at dawn.

Hareera is often taken for breakfast at other times during the year. In the market places, such as at Marrakech, in the early, mountain-cool mornings, one will see tables set out in the open with large bowls stacked on them, and alongside, the steaming cauldron of soup. Westerners resident here know and acclaim the rich, thick, creamy soup. It makes an excellent one-dish lunch, or a fine soup course for dinner.

Moroccans from different parts of the country are unanimous in their appreciation of hareera but its style of preparation is acceptable to each only 'the way my mother does it', or the way it is customarily made in his own locality. We give several recipes, one as good as the other.

Hareera
(Serves 6–8)

Chicken is the prescribed meat base for the true hareera and imparts the best flavour – but veal or beef of any cut may be used.

STEP 1 Put in deep soup pot:

$\frac{1}{2}$ lb raw chicken, cut up very small

1 cup chick-peas (which have soaked overnight)

1 cup onion, diced

1 cup parsley, minced

$\frac{1}{4}$ cup butter

2 teaspoons black pepper

$\frac{1}{4}$ teaspoon saffron

2 tablespoons salt

1 heaped teaspoon cinnamon (optional)

Stir ingredients over a fast fire for 2 minutes; then add:

$3\frac{1}{2}$ quarts hot water

Cook for 1 hour – until chicken and chick-peas are done.

STEP 2 Now add into soup pot:

$\frac{1}{2}$ cup rice (or $\frac{1}{2}$ cup fine crushed noodles)

Continue cooking until rice or noodles are tender. If hareera is not to be served in the next few minutes, remove from fire and continue preparation, after reheating, just before serving. Up until now, more water may be added if desired, but not later.

STEP 3 When rice or noodles are cooked, very slowly and stirring constantly, add in a thin smooth mixture of:

   ⅓ cup flour
   ¾ cup water

Rinse flour bowl with another cup of water and add this too, mixing in well with the soup. Lower flame and continue cooking, stirring the soup lazily for the next 15 minutes; then remove from fire.

STEP 4 With soup off fire, add into it slowly, stirring all the time:

   3 raw eggs, slightly beaten

Mix in well. The heat in the soup cooks eggs. Allow hareera to stand 5 minutes before serving.

SERVE by taking a cupful of solid ingredients from the bottom of pot, and a cupful of liquid from the surface. Hareera is best served in bowls. Squeeze lemon juice generously over servings. *Note: The lemon juice is important to hareera.* Dates and dried figs are often eaten along with this – all around dish. It is not recommended to drink anything, either wine, beer or water, with it.

Hareera (2)

The country people make a heavier soup, using both noodles and rice in Step 2, as well as chick-peas in Step 1. It is also very good.

Hareera (3)

Mrs Abdullah, a city resident in Tangier, insists that both hareera 1 and 2 are too heavy, and that *this* is the right way to make it. Eliminate chick-peas and cinnamon from Step 1, and in their stead put:

   2 cups mashed tomatoes

The other ingredients in Step 1 remain unaltered. She cooks the tomatoes slowly for 20 minutes, stirring constantly until the ingredients are like a purée. Then she adds:

   3 quarts water

Step 2 corresponds to the basic recipe. She prefers her flour-water mixture in Step 3 to have been soured overnight but if she has forgotten to put it aside she mixes it at the time of cooking.

Hareera (4)

Mohammed J., an artist who hails from Fez where some of the best foods are prepared, insists that the *true* hareera is made in the Fezzi manner. His mother begins the preparation of it the night before it is to be eaten.

She leaves a thin mixture of flour and water set in a bowl overnight to slightly sour. Also overnight, a huge pot containing 6 to 8 quarts of water and chicken bones is left to simmer lazily over the charcoal fire.

In the morning chicken bones and stock are strained through a very fine cloth to remove bones and any splinters. Eliminating the cinnamon, the ingredients and the procedure in Step 1 are the same as in the basic recipe Hareera 1. In adding water, only the amount required to make up the difference between bones broth and the necessary $3\frac{1}{2}$ quarts is added.

To the flour-water mixture in Step 3, a pounded mixture of a handful of parsley, a stalk of fresh cardamon, and $\frac{1}{4}$ teaspoon saffron are added. The mixture turns green and is then added slowly to soup, which from then on is stirred constantly. The raw eggs are added finally, just before serving, as in Hareera 1.

Our preference in hareera? We suggest you try each one – they are all excellent.

ULK'TBAN
(*Pinchitos*)

Recipe for a barbecue

Beef, veal, lamb or mutton may be used for making succulent and inexpensive brochette or pinchitos (bits of meat on a skewer), and of these just about every cut such as kidney, heart, liver, may be included. They are to North Africa what hamburgers and hot-dogs are to America – and similarly to be found at street-stands . . . Western hostesses find them not only fun to make and serve but also economical as lesser amounts of meat are required than to serve steaks.

The perfume of sizzling barbecued meat emanates from lean-tos in the *souks* all year round, but the dish is traditional for the first day of Aid-el-Kebir. This feast marks the end of the pilgrimage to Mecca and is celebrated throughout the Islamic world, at which time the head of every Moslem family must sacrifice a sheep.

Beginning two days before the Feast, sheep and rams fill the streets of the towns as they are herded to and from market. Their stubborn gait and plaintive bleat seem to show they know what awaits them. I shall always remember the picture of two Arab countrymen driving a flock of five up the sidewalk in midtown Tangier on a hot summer afternoon. The animals baulked just under the shade of a shop awning, and no amount of pushing or beating would move them. The man in the rear gave up, mopped his brow and the whole party sat down to rest on the pavement, while passers-by, smiling, encouraged them with: '*Allah eowin*' ('God give you strength to carry on') – or 'God will reward you for all your pains'. (Moroccans talk freely with one another even when they are strangers, and more so at this time when a holiday spirit such as we know at Christmas pervades the air.) Another common sight is the man who has lost patience with the animal and, picking it up, slings it over his shoulder, and carries it home.

After the animal is killed, the first meat removed in the cleaning is the liver, which is immediately cut up in small pieces, skewered and barbecued for lunch. The tripe is used for supper. Such parts are good only when very fresh. The rest of the animal is usually cured for a few days before eating.

Pinchitos (1)

This recipe may be applied to beef or mutton, using meat and/or liver, kidney and heart. Two lbs are ample for 6 people. Cube meat in ½" bite-size pieces. Cube in tiny pieces ¼ lb of suet, or fat.

STEP 1 Pound into a paste in the mortar:
½ head garlic, peeled
5 tablespoons parsley, minced
1 tablespoon salt
3 – 4 teaspoons cumin seed, ground
1 teaspoon hot red pepper pods

STEP 2 Blend meat and suet together with spice paste in a dish and allow to marinate 15 or 20 minutes. Then spit alternately bits of meat with bits of suet on skewers.

Hold skewers of meat over hot smokeless wood or charcoal embers, or rest ends in such a way that they do not touch the embers. Turn over when done on one side. Lacking such fuel, they may be done in oven by resting ends of skewers on the edges of a roasting pan.

SERVE Hot, with or without pinchito hot sauce, on individual plates. Moroccans eat them by gripping the skewer in one hand and drawing off each bit of meat with the other together with a bit of bread. They must be eaten hot and while on the skewer may easily be returned to coals for reheating. A side dish of radishes and olives should accompany.

Mutton Pinchitos (2)

A completely distinct flavour is achieved by using mutton (only) with a different set of spices. Recipe applies to 2½ lbs mutton (leg or other boneless, tender cut) and ¼ lb suet. Cube in 1" squares, or better yet, have the butcher do it.

STEP 1 Pound into a paste in the mortar:
    1 cup onion, diced fine
    ½ cup parsley, minced
    1 tablespoon salt
    1 teaspoon black pepper
    Blend spices with meat and suet and leave to marinate for 15 minutes. Then spit meat and suet alternately on skewers. Roast barbecue style over smokeless hot coals of wood or charcoal.

SERVE On plates or on skewers, with or without hot sauce. *Variation:* seasoned simply with salt and crushed cumin seed pinchitos are still delicious.

Hamburger Pinchitos (3)
'L'Kifta Mtoona'

Moroccans put meat through the grinder twice; the first time with suet, the second laced with the spices. We prefer to have the butcher grind it very fine and add the spices ourselves. Recipe takes care of 2¼ lbs ground, beef, veal or mutton and ½ lb suet, also ground.

STEP 1 Prepare first, then blend thoroughly with meat and suet:
    ¼ cup onion, minced
    ½ cup parsley, minced
    1 teaspoon black pepper
    1 teaspoon sweet red pepper
    juice of 1 lemon
    1 tablespoon salt

STEP 2 First wetting the hand (this is important), mould the meat lengthwise onto wire skewers to about ¾" thickness. Barbecue over hot smokeless coals of wood or charcoal. Do not allow flames to scorch meat.

Pinchito Hot Sauce

STEP 1 Pound in the mortar:
    1 head of garlic, peeled

5 tablespoons parsley, minced
1 teaspoon cumin seed, crushed
1 teaspoon hot red peppers
1 teaspoon sweet red pepper

STEP 2 Blend together:
$\frac{1}{2}$ cup lemon juice (or light vinegar)
$\frac{1}{4}$ cup oil
2 cups water
salt to taste
1 lemon (or lime) including rind, diced very fine. If
preserved lemon is on hand, use that.

Combine Step 1 and Step 2 ingredients. To add an extra touch,
toss in:

1 cup black or green olives

SERVE Sauce in a bowl at table, letting each person help himself.
Some *don't* like it hot.

BASTELA

(*Pastilla*)

🙰

Pigeon Pie

'There are two kinds of people in this world,' says Shereef, 'those who have eaten bastela, and those other unfortunates who have not.'

Most people would agree that bastela is one of the most succulent and delicious of dishes anywhere, a food fit for the angels. It may not have inspired 'the four and twenty blackbirds baked in a pie', but it is surely a dish to set before a king. It takes the longest time of any found here to prepare and it is worth the time.

Wrapped in rich, gossamer-fine, flaky pastry, the filling is a blend of boned chicken (or doves), with parsley and egg which have been pre-prepared along with oil and spices. Although historians credit Syria with originating it, the people of Fez claim the honour of producing the best example of it.

The Fezzi (from Fez) put the ingredients together loosely, leaving the boned meat in large juicy morsels; in Marrakech it is sweetened by sprinkling crushed sugar over the top crust, and the filling contains eggs under-hardboiled. In Tangier all possible filling ingredients are packed firmly into a solid mass before being wrapped in pastry leaves. A woman from Oujda would throw up her hands at all these; bastela for her must be of dove meat, parsley and eggs, with a layer of ground almonds on the bottom crust.

Whether it be from Fez or Tangier, Oujda or Marrakech, bastela is the pride of the Moroccan kitchen. Its praises, documented by travellers and historians, justly approach the ecstatic. It is a rich dish, for the rich in appreciation, and customarily is served as a first course in a Moroccan *diffa*.

We suggest that most Western cooks will want to use puff paste – or other rich pastry shell, inasmuch as the pastry part made in the Moroccan manner takes several hours. Time in Morocco is less closely rationed than in other parts of the world and this and the fact there are many hands to help probably accounts for the Moroccan women being such excellent cooks.

The way the Moroccan makes pastry for bastela merits trying if one has the time. The idea is to achieve a tissue-fine and feather-light crust. The dough itself is made of only flour, salt and water as in standard dough, and is kneaded on such hard surfaces as brass or marble for some time until fluffy.

A metal sheet is used, or a clean empty frying tin turned upside down, and is layed over a slow flame for baking the pastry. The dough is then wetted with water, and mixed with the water until rather sticky.

Taking a ball of the wetted dough in the right hand, the cook, in a darting quick motion, dabs the overturned pan with it, quickly and immediately lifting the dough away, so that literally the metal is lightly kissed by the dough. This is repeated over and over, in dots and dabs, all over the area of the pan until a trans-parent gossamer thin crust is formed. When a layer is formed, it is lifted off carefully, and another begun. This is continued until some 60 to 80 fine leaves are formed. They need not be perfect squares or rounds.

Bastela is rather expensive and time-consuming to make, so we suggest these proportions for two (standard pie size) to make it worth while. There should then be enough to serve a large party, or to keep one in the refrigerator for later use. Like apple or mincemeat pie, bastela can be reheated. The recipe should be halved, for just one serving for six, using a little more than half the liquid measurements.

Bastela Filling (1)
From Fez

STEP 1 Put together in deep casserole:
     5 lbs chicken, pigeon or squab (cut up to facilitate cooking)
     giblets
     2½–3 cups onion, diced coarsely
     2 cups parsley, diced fine
     1 small sprig fresh cardamon, if available
     1 teaspoon black pepper

½ teaspoon ginger
¼ teaspoon nutmeg
1 tablespoon cinnamon
½ teaspoon powdered saffron
2 teaspoons salt
1 tablespoon butter
1 pint olive oil

Cover and set on high fire for 10 minutes. Stir often (or as Moroccans do, hold the lid on tight with both hands and shake the pot), so that ingredients mix well. After 15 minutes, when the flesh is golden and has pretty well absorbed the spices, add:

1 quart hot water

Recover and continue cooking until meat is tender. Remove meat from broth and bone it.

Continue cooking the stock until only the oily mixture remains. All water must be cooked off.

STEP 2 Lay the bottom pastry layer (formed in the Moroccan manner by 10 thicknesses of pastry leaves, with each leaf oiled from the oil in casserole) on an oiled baking sheet. Distribute the pieces of boned meat loosely, and not packed together, around on the surface of the pastry. Sprinkle lightly with drops of the oil.

STEP 3 When meat has been distributed around on the pastry, reheat the remaining oil mixture to a simmer. Add in:
10 broken raw eggs
Stir slowly until egg white shows white and slightly cooked.

STEP 4 Take teaspoonsful of the onion-egg-parsley mixture from the oil and distribute them around between and over the pieces of meat. Sprinkle several tablespoons of the oil from the casserole over all.

STEP 5 Form the top layer of the pastry (ten thicknesses of pastry, each leaf oiled) laying one atop and over-lapping. Fold the edges of the top pastry layer down over the tart, and the bottom layer up over this. Sprinkle the top with oil. Seal sides with egg white (never with water). Sprinkle top with the oil.

STEP 6 Put baking sheet with bastela on it in pre-heated oven, leave until slightly browned. Lift carefully with a spatula to check against burning and spoon in more oil underneath if needed. (Pastry must not break.)

If ordinary pie-pastry or puff paste are used with usual pie pan or oven baking dish, first oil the tin or glass well with oil stock. Proceed in same manner as in Fez style to lay in the filling. Sprinkle the surface of bottom crust thinly with oil stock. In covering the pastry, sprinkle the top and seal edges with oil stock and finish to light brown in oven.

Variation An even richer bastela can be made by spreading a fine layer of finely-chopped, blanched and very lightly toasted almonds between the first and second leaves of the bottom crust.

SERVE Warm. Sugar and cinnamon may be sprinkled on top, according to individual tastes.

Bastela Filling
Tangier Style

STEP 1 Follow Step 1 of Fez style, except to reduce the quantities of parsley and onion by half. When cooked, set aside ½ cup of broth for moistening pastry later.

STEP 2 Apart, when Step 1 is finished, add together:
3 cups chicken broth
2 cups parsley, chopped very fine
2 cups onion, diced very fine

Cook in saucepan until onion is tender, adding chicken broth if mixture goes dry before onion is cooked. Leave simmer until onion is cooked and mixture is practically dry, like a paste.

STEP 3 Add together in a large bowl:
the cooked meat, boned and shredded
the parsley-onion mixture
1 dozen hard-boiled eggs, crushed or cubed
3 tablespoons cinnamon
juice of 1 lemon

Blend all together well by hand, and turn out in a solid mass on pastry shell dotted with butter.

STEP 4 Finish in oven on baking sheet or in pie tin, as in Bastela No. 1.

(Substitute Step 2: If one prefers to proceed without waiting for chicken to cook, the onion-parsley paste may be made thus: Add together in saucepan:

  $\frac{1}{2}$ cup olive oil
  2 cups parsley, minced
  2 cups onion, minced
  1 tablespoon cinnamon
  1 teaspoon black pepper
  2 teaspoons salt
  1 quart warm water

Cook until onion is thoroughly done and mixture is practically dry.)

FRACKH
(or *Schena*)
✕⟨◦⟩✕

(Baked bean pot. Serves 8 or more)

Frackh is a Saturday dish, for it is the Sabbath dinner of the Moroccan Jews. A considerable and important element in the country, the Jews have a long history here. Those who arrived in the eighth century and those exiled from Spain in the fifteenth century found their co-religionists already here; indeed, Jewish colonies were here when the first Arabs arrived in 681, which gives rise to the conjecture that they may have been direct descendants of one of the 'lost tribes'.

Like the country Arab, they have preserved all the old traditions, and being extremely orthodox, strictly observe the old laws, amongst which is forbidden the building of a fire on the Sabbath. Orthodox Jews in Morocco eat frackh every Saturday of their lives and to the exclusion of all other foods. Other Moroccan families prepare it once or twice a month.

The frackh pot is made ready Friday afternoon, and then one can see the huge pots carried through the streets to the local baker's oven. Left in the oven overnight, it slowly cooks to a juicy brown in the intense heat accumulated there.

For cooking in the oven, a pot big enough to hold 6 to 8 quarts of water is necessary. With the ingredients placed in it, the lid is sealed on with flour and water, making it the original pressure cooker. Some families do cook it at home, very slowly atop a charcoal stove, from four p.m. Friday afternoon until the next morning. (Charcoals glow for a long time, and should they burn out, a servant of another religion may rekindle them.)

Cooking atop the stove produces a tastier dish than that done in the oven. A very large casserole is needed. With the use of gas or electricity, cooking time can be reduced to 4–5 hours.

Frackh (1)

STEP 1 Singe off hair and wash well:
2 calves feet (or oxen or cow) – this to include foot, ankle, lower shank

STEP 2 Place in deep pot, one over the other:

the bones and meat (bones to be cracked)	1 tablespoon salt
1 cup dry beans, any kind	1 tablespoon ground cumin seed
1 cup chick-peas (first soaked overnight)	½ teaspoon hot red peppers, cut up
1 cup parsley, chopped fine	2 tablespoons sweet red pepper (or paprika)
4 whole heads garlic (not peeled)	1 cup hot olive oil
6 whole raw potatoes, peeled	5 cups cold water (poured over)
1 egg, unbroken, for each person	

STEP 3 Do not mix ingredients. Cover pot tightly and cook over medium-high heat. After about an hour, add 3 cups water, after the second hour, 3 more cups water. Much more water is not necessary if lid is on tight. Total cooking time of four hours produces a good dish, but the longer cooked, the better. One may choose to finish the last half hour in the oven. The consistency will be much like that of other baked beans – but the taste lent by the bones and spices is special.

Frackh (2)

Dafina
(for 6)

This is one of the dishes which falls under the general heading of frackh, meaning 'happiness', and which is prepared on Friday afternoons for eating on Hebrew Sabbath. The recipe comes from Mogador, a city on the southern Atlantic coast, and the oldest and most indigenously Jewish city in Morocco.

STEP 1 Put together in large deep casserole 8–10 quart size:
½ lb fatty meat (beef or veal)

1½ cups dried beans (soaked overnight)
6 eggs, unbroken
6–8 peeled whole potatoes
1 tablespoon black pepper
½ teaspoon saffron
1 tablespoon cinnamon
2 tablespoons salt
1 tablespoon caramelized sugar
1 cup warm oil
water to cover

Set over steady low fire. Keep covered, but check occasionally to see if more water is needed. Moroccans let this cook atop the stove for 20 hours. However, good results may be obtained by cooking four or five hours, though the longer it is cooked the better and tastier it is.

Orissa

Three cups of wheat have been used in the following recipe which is also a kind of frackh. However, the wheat content may alter as long as 2 parts water are used to 1 part wheat. The husks of the wheat must first be rubbed off.

STEP 1 Put together in a large deep pot:

3 cups wheat
6 cups water
1 cup oil
1 tablespoon hot red peppers
1 tablespoon sweet red pepper
2 heads garlic, peeled
1 tablespoon caramelized sugar
2 tablespoons salt
1 lb fatty breast of beef
1 egg, unbroken, per person
small peeled new potatoes (optional)

It is important that no air enter the pot. Seal lid to pot with flour-water paste. In Morocco, the pot rests in the baker's oven overnight. I would suggest cooking it at home overnight on a low flame or in slow oven.

MINT TEA

(*Etzay*)

The first act – the traditional mark of hospitality – which takes place when friend, family or stranger crosses the threshold of a Moroccan home is the preparation and serving of hot mint tea. And you will show your appreciation by drinking as many as three full glasses. It is refreshing at all times, comforting in cold damp weather, and the best finale to a large meal. Mint tea is not a packaged item here. Anyone with a mint patch can offer this brew to guests at a moment's notice, for it is made simply of green China tea and fresh mint leaves.

Just about the most important piece of furniture a bride takes to her new home is the teatable. If she is poor, it will be a small wooden tray two feet in diameter and set on three six-inch legs. Country people buy them unpainted and often trace on them colourful geometric designs. In a wealthy home, it may be bigger, more ornate, of brass or copper. Equipment consists of the teapot and sugar bowl in silver, chrome or tin, and many small thin glasses. Tea and sugar are two of the biggest imports in North Africa.

Tea is at least as much a tradition here as in England. The countryman will stop while travelling by camel or burro to brew a pot. Luggage for an afternoon on the beach includes the tea tray just as it does the thermos flask in other latitudes. No reunion is complete without it, and men do much of their visiting during the long hours of business over a pot of tea; no self-respecting shopkeeper would be without the necessary paraphernalia in the back of his establishment, ready to provide hospitality to his friends or any sympathetic stranger who wanders in.

The first time I drank mint tea, I sat on a rug on the ground and huddled, along with several others, against the wall of an old mosque to break the chill wind coming off the Algerian Sahara. The next time was in the shop of a rug merchant, when between us we settled the ills of the world with homey philosophy over the three prescribed glasses. Nor would it have occurred to him to be offended when I left without buying.

Tea-making is a ritual, accomplished in the following manner:
Put one after the other in a teapot of about 1 quart capacity:

$\frac{1}{2}$ dessertspoon green China tea

3 cups boiling water

3 dessertspoons sugar

1 handful mint leaves (leaves only), pushed well to bottom
with a spoon

Slowly pour boiling water – enough to fill up the pot – from the
height of a foot or more above the teapot.

If orange blossoms are available, the addition of the petals (only)
of five or six blossoms makes the tea especially fragrant and
delightful. Or add 2 tablespoons orange blossom water. Lacking
both these, the finely peeled orange part of a mandarin or tangerine
rind may be added.

Mix the tea well in the pot with a silver spoon. Fill a thin glass
with tea, then pour it back in the pot. The tea-brewer then usually
pours out $\frac{1}{4}$ glassful and samples it for taste and sweetness, before
pouring.

SERVE   Very, very hot. Or once made, it may be drained, removing
tea and mint leaves and kept in a cool place for a hot
weather refresher.

THE
REPERTOIRE

SOUPS

Giblet Soup
L'Hamraak
(Serves 6)

STEP 1 Put in soup casserole:
> ½ cup chick-peas (which have soaked overnight)
> 2 cups tomatoes, peeled and crushed
> giblets, necks, etc. of pigeons, chickens, or other fowl
> ¾ cup onion, diced fine
> 1 stalk fresh cardamon (if available)
> a few stalks of parsley
> 1 tablespoon salt
> ½ teaspoon cinnamon
> ½ teaspoon black pepper
> ¼ cup butter
> 1 teaspoon saffron
> sufficient water to just barely cover

Cover with lid and cook over medium-high fire until the pot is almost dry. Then add:
> 6 cups hot water

Continue simmering until meat is tender.

Note If soup is being prepared much before it is to be eaten, do not take the next steps until a few minutes before it is to be served. Then proceed with:

STEP 2 Add into the boiling soup:
> ½ cup very fine noodles (or vermicelli)

Bring all to a boil once. Then add a medium-light thickening of:
> 1 cup water
> ¼ cup flour

Rinse flour bowl and add this water also into soup pot. Stir in well. After 2 minutes, remove pot from fire.

STEP 3 Apart, blend well together:
> 2 raw eggs
> juice of 1 lemon
> ¼ cup soup stock

Turn above into soup, stirring well. The heat in the soup cooks the egg.

SERVE Immediately.

Beef Soup
L'Hamraak
(Serves 6)

STEP I Add together in soup pot:
   $\frac{1}{2}$ lb soup beef, coarsely cubed
   $\frac{1}{2}$ cup lentils (which have soaked an hour)
   1 cup onion, diced fine
   $\frac{1}{4}$ cup celery, including leaves, cut up
   $\frac{1}{2}$ cup parsley, minced
   1 teaspoon black pepper
   1 tablespoon cinnamon
   $\frac{1}{2}$ teaspoon powdered saffron
   $\frac{1}{4}$ cup butter
   1 tablespoon salt
   $2\frac{1}{2}$ quarts water

Simmer over medium-high fire until lentils are done. Then add:
   $\frac{1}{2}$ cup uncooked rice

Soup is ready when rice is cooked.

SERVE Hot, with a slice of lemon.

Moroccan Bisque
L'Hamraak Hfeef

STEP I Add together in soup pot:
   2 cups carrots, cubed
   1 cup onion, cubed
   2 cups turnips (or potatoes), cubed
   $\frac{1}{2}$ cup parsley, chopped fine
   $\frac{1}{4}$ cup butter
   1 lb bones
   $\frac{1}{2}$ teaspoon black pepper
   1 teaspoon cinnamon
   1 tablespoon salt

sufficient water to just cover and prevent burning, but very little

Cook until vegetables are tender.

STEP 2 Remove bones. Pass vegetables *and* stock through sieve or food mill.

STEP 3 Reheat soup to under boiling point. Then add in over the fire:

1½ cups milk

Stir well over heat until sufficiently hot. Do not allow soup to boil.

SERVE Hot, immediately, garnished with minced parsley or paprika.

Spaghetti Soup

Shareeyah L'Hamraak

(Serves 6)

STEP 1 Bring to a boil:

1 quart milk
1 pint water
1 teaspoon salt

When liquid boils, add:

3 cups very fine spaghetti, crushed
1 tablespoon butter

SERVE When spaghetti is cooked. Sugar and cinnamon may be sprinkled on top

FISH

Fish and Carrots
L'Hootz Bijada
(Serves 6)

This is an excellent way to dress up any inexpensive grade of fish.
Ingredients here suffice to prepare 3 lbs – allowing $\frac{1}{2}$ lb per person.

STEP 1 Boil together in salted water:
  2 cups carrots, cubed coarsely
  2 cups potatoes, „   „
When cooked, drain and set aside, but keep 1 cup of the liquid.

STEP 2 Pound into a paste in mortar:
  1 tablespoon garlic, diced fine
  $\frac{1}{2}$ cup parsley, chopped fine
  $\frac{1}{2}$ teaspoon salt
  1 teaspoon ground cumin seed
  $\frac{1}{2}$ teaspoon hot red chili peppers

STEP 3 Put, in layers one atop the other in wide shallow saucepan
  or frying pan:
  1 large onion, sliced
  several stalks of parsley
  the fish, cut in crosswise portions
  1 teaspoon black pepper
  1 tablespoon salt
Cover fish with cold water and parboil for 10 minutes.

STEP 4 Melt in saucepan:
  $\frac{1}{4}$ cup butter
Add into butter over fire, mixing well:
  spice paste (Step 2)
  potatoes and carrots (Step 1)
  1 cup water (from potatoes and carrots)
When liquid boils, remove the potatoes and carrots; lay fish in the
liquid. Leave on medium fire 10 minutes.

SERVE On large serving platter, fish garnished with potatoes and
  carrots. Squeeze drops of lemon juice over all.

Swordfish Stew

L'Hootz F'Tadjeen

(Serves 4)

Other similar dry, meaty fish may be used to make excellent stew. Put one atop the other in layers in casserole:

1 lb fish, cut in chunks

1 cup onion, sliced thin lengthwise

1 teaspoon *lacama* (equal proportions: cinnamon, black pepper, curry, ginger, nutmeg)

1 cup potatoes and carrots, diced

1 cup tomatoes, crushed or cubed fine

1 tablespoon salt

1 teaspoon sweet red pepper

$\frac{1}{2}$ teaspoon saffron

Lastly, over all, pour:

$\frac{1}{2}$ cup heated olive oil

If available, place on top:

1 sweet red pimento

Simmer slowly for about $\frac{3}{4}$ hour. Do not mix.

SERVE Hot, with drops of lemon juice

Baked Fish

L'Hootz Shkfah

This recipe may be used for flounder, haddock, hake, whiting, cod, rockfish, or any lean, dry-meated fish other than sole. The proportions given here are adequate for preparing $2\frac{1}{2}$ lbs of fish.

STEP 1 Clean fish, cut off head and tail of each, but otherwise leave whole. Gash each fish cross-wise on but do not cut clear through.

STEP 2 Mix and crush the following into a paste in mortar:

1 tablespoon ground cumin seed

1 tablespoon salt

1 teaspoon hot red peppers

1 head garlic, peeled

$\frac{2}{3}$ cup parsley, minced

Fill the gashes and cavity of fish with spice paste.

STEP 3 Cover surface of roasting platter with:
     sliced raw potatoes

Place fish on top of potato layer. Distribute around and between fish:
     2 to 3 tomatoes, sliced lengthwise
     1 onion, sliced lengthwise
     sliced lemon rings

STEP 4 Pour over the fish, a mixture of:
     $\frac{2}{3}$ cup olive oil
     1 tablespoon sweet red pepper

Then pour evenly over the platter:
     2 cups water

Sprinkle with:
     1 teaspoon salt

STEP 5 Put in preheated oven or under broiler. When potatoes are done (approx. $\frac{1}{2}$ hour), dish is ready.

SERVE Hot, sprinkled with lemon juice; add quartered lemons for extra garnish.

Fish Barbeque
L'Hootz Mischui

Small, scaleless fish, such as sardines, are best for barbecuing. Clean, remove entrails, gills, fins and any scales of fish. Spit fish through the sides on skewer and roast over smokeless wood fire or hot charcoals.

SERVE Dressed with salt, oil, vinegar and minced parsley.

Fish Roast
L'Hootz Mtayeeb

This recipe gives excellent results applied to almost any fish, but the firmer the flesh the better. It requires 2–3 lbs of fish.

STEP 1 Scale and clean fish; cut off tail and remove gills, but otherwise leave whole with the head on. Gash each side crosswise several times, but without cutting clear through.

STEP 2 Pound into a paste in the mortar:

1 head of garlic, peeled
½ cup parsley, minced
1 tablespoon ground cumin seed
½ teaspoon hot red chili peppers
1 tablespoon salt

STEP 3 Fill cavity and gashes on fish with spice paste.

STEP 4 Place fish on roasting rack over smokeless wood fire or hot charcoals – or under preheated grill. A flat baking dish may be used if frequently basted with oil or butter. Remove from heat when thoroughly roasted and golden.

SERVE Hot, with lemon juice squeezed over it.

Grilled Fish Steaks
L'Hootz Fufarran

This recipe may be applied to any dry-meated, firm-fleshed fish such as swordfish, cod, sturgeon, salmon, haddock, etc.

STEP 1 Cut cleaned fish in steaks. Soak for a few minutes in water with salt and vinegar. Rinse in clear water and blot dry.

STEP 2 Crush into a paste in mortar:
1 tablespoon parsley, minced
1 tablespoon garlic, diced
1 teaspoon salt
1 teaspoon ground cumin seed
2 teaspoons rosemary

Rub spice paste all over each portion of fish.

STEP 3 Melt together in shallow roasting pan:
2 tablespoons butter
1 tablespoon oil
¼ teaspoon salt

Lay fish in pan, baste with liquid, and add:
2 tablespoons water

Place under medium hot grill until done.

SERVE Hot, with drops of lemon juice *or* with Tomato Sauce (see p. 68.)

Herring Stew
L'Hootz Ftadjeen
(Serves 4–5)

Mackerel or other similar fish may also be used for making this stew which is a Jewish dish from Mogador. Recipe requires 2 lbs fish and will serve 4 to 5 people.

STEP 1 Bring slowly to a boil in frying pan:
⅓ cup olive oil
When oil bubbles, add:
    1 teaspoon sweet red pepper (paprika)
    1 cup water
Let boil ten minutes, then remove any sediment.

STEP 2 Place in casserole one atop the other in layers:
    the fish, cut in large chunks
    1 teaspoon coriander, chopped
    20 cloves of garlic, unpeeled
    1 cup bread crumbs
    1 teaspoon salt
    the oil from Step 1
Cover and cook over a slow fire for 20–30 minutes.

Swordfish with Tomato Sauce
L'Hootz Bcharmeela Mneedan Ltaff

This recipe may be made with any other dry, firm-fleshed fish. It's the sauce which makes it a regular favourite.

The Sauce
STEP 1 Preheat in saucepan or large frying pan:
½ cup olive oil
When oil is hot, add one after the other quickly, and stirring in:
    1 tablespoon sweet red pepper (or paprika)
    ½ cup water
    1 teaspoon salt
Then add, all at once:
    1 tablespoon garlic, peeled and sliced
    1 teaspoon ground cumin seed

½ teaspoon hot red chili peppers
½ cup parsley, minced
2 cups tomatoes, mashed or cubed
½ lemon including rind, diced
    (Use preserved lemon, page 128, if it is on hand.)
Mix altogether well over the fire, then add:
    1 cup water
Continue cooking over fast fire, stirring constantly, for 10 minutes.
Remove from fire and pass all through a sieve or food mill. The
sauce is now ready for use, now or later. Reheat before serving,
and add a few drops of lemon juice.

The Fish

STEP 2 Slice fish into steaks. Wash and soak a few minutes in
water to which a little salt and vinegar have been added.
Drain and wash lightly in water. Blot dry. Dredge fish
lightly in flour with a pinch of salt. Sautée in a little
preheated oil or butter.

SERVE Hot, with sauce over fish.

Fried Fish
L'Hootz Muklee

This recipe may be applied to flounder, haddock, hake, whiting,
etc., or any similar lean, dry-meated fish. Proportions here are
sufficient to prepare 3 or more pounds of fish – for 6 persons.

STEP 1 Scale and clean fish, remove heads and tails. Cut fish in
portions by cutting crosswise through the backbone. Gash
the meaty sides of each portion once or twice, but do not
cut clear through.

STEP 2 Pound into a paste in the mortar:
    2 teaspoons ground cumin seed
    1 scant tablespoon salt
    2 stalks rosemary
    1 teaspoon hot red peppers
    1 head garlic, peeled
    ¼ cup parsley, minced
    1 teaspoon vinegar

STEP 3 Fill gashes and rub each portion with spice paste. Then leave to marinate 20 or 30 minutes.

STEP 4 Dredge fish lightly in a mixture of:
½ cup flour
1 tablespoon paprika

STEP 5 Fry fish in ¼ cup of preheated olive oil.

SERVE Hot, with lemon juice *or* accompanied by Carrot Salad (p. 103) *or* Tomato Sauce (p. 68).

SHELLFISH

Shrimp Omelet
(Serves 4)

STEP 1 Drop 1 pound or more shrimps in boiling water and leave for a minute or two to cook slightly. Drain, cool, peel.

STEP 2 Heat in frying pan:
   3 tablespoons olive oil
When oil is hot (but not boiling), add:
   1 tablespoon garlic, sliced fine
When garlic is toasted a very light golden, add quickly, one after the other, and distributing evenly over surface of pan:
   the shrimps
   2 tablespoons parsley, minced
   1 teaspoon ground cumin seed
   ½ teaspoon salt
   4 eggs, beaten
When egg is set but slightly undercooked, fold over, and remove from fire.

SERVE Hot, garnished with finely chopped parsley. Moroccans sprinkle sugar over the top. (For individual servings, quarter the recipe.)

Shrimp Omelet with Almonds
(A one-dish lunch, or dessert for 4)

STEP 1 Prepare 1 lb shrimps by dropping in boiling water for a few minutes; drain, cool and peel.

STEP 2 Heat in wide frying pan:
   ⅓ cup olive oil
Add to hot oil, mixing over fire:
   4 tablespoons onion, minced
When onion is golden, add quickly, one after the other and sprinkling evenly over the surface:

4 heaped tablespoons parsley, minced
½ teaspoon ground cumin seed
the shrimps
½ cup blanched, skinned and slightly toasted almonds, chopped fine
1 heaped tablespoon sugar
4 beaten eggs

When egg is set, sprinkle lightly with sugar, and/or crushed almonds.

SERVE Hot in wedges. For individual servings, use a very small frying pan and just a quarter of each ingredient.

Mussels
Sstrmbak

Three cups of the meat serves 6. Excellent as an appetizer or with aperitif.

STEP 1 Clean mussels very well and put in deep pot or casserole. Cover with water. Add:
2 tablespoons salt

Bring to a boil. When shells open, drain and cool. Remove meat from shells.

STEP 2 Mix together:
¼ cup onion, diced very fine
1 cup tomatoes, diced fine
½ cup parsley, chopped fine
½ teaspoon hot red peppers
1 teaspoon sweet red pepper
1 teaspoon ground cumin seed
1 tablespoon salt

STEP 3 Heat in saucepan or frying pan:
½ cup olive oil

Add: spice mixture from Step 2
½ cup water

Bring liquid and spices to a boil, then add:
mussel meat

Continue cooking for 10 minutes. Remove from fire, cool.

SERVE Cool with some of liquid and a few drops of lemon and

¼ of a lemon rind diced very fine. If preserved lemon is on hand, use it instead.

Clams
L'Mah Harh

Excellent with aperitif. If using as an appetizer, allow 2 cups of whole clams per person. Wash and clean shellfish well.

STEP 1 Heat in frying pan:
½ cup olive oil
Put clams in hot oil, and mix constantly until shells open.

STEP 2 Add to clams in oil:
1 teaspoon hot red pepper
1 teaspoon paprika
2 tablespoons parsley, minced
1 teaspoon salt
½ cup water
1 tablespoon garlic, diced fine
When liquid again boils, add:
½ cup water
(Although Moroccans do not use wine in cooking, we suggest this last ½ cup water be replaced with ½ cup white wine.)
Cook 5 minutes more – or until liquid again boils. Remove clams from liquid.

SERVE Hot with a little of the sauce and some lemon juice.

FOWL

Chicken with Onion and Parsley
Sjdeda Bi Madnoos

STEP 1 Bathe chicken, or chickens, in a mixture of:
>   1 tablespoon salt
>   ½ teaspoon saffron
>   ¼ cup hot water

Pour into the cavity any remaining liquid. Tuck legs of chicken into cavity.

STEP 2 Put in casserole:
>   the chicken
>   ⅔ cup butter (or margarine)
>   1 teaspoon black pepper
>   a few slices of onion

Cover casserole tightly with lid and set on high fire. After a minute or two, add:
>   1 cup olive oil

Continue cooking, stirring well and turning chicken over for about 15 minutes, when chicken will have absorbed most of the liquid. Then add:
>   6 cups hot water

Continue cooking more slowly, with lid on, for about an hour. Remove lid then to step up evaporation, and continue cooking for 15–20 minutes more. Chicken should be done then, with the liquid only about an inch deep in pot.

Onion-Parsley Dressing
Apart, while chicken cooks, add together:
>   1½ cups parsley, minced
>   1½ cups onion, minced
>   2 tablespoons butter
>   ½ teaspoon black pepper
>   ½ teaspoon saffron
>   1 teaspoon salt

Wilt the above in covered saucepan over low fire. Check and stir occasionally. After about 15 minutes, when onion and parsley are limp, add in:

4 tablespoons chicken broth

Mix well, and continue cooking. Add more broth if mixture goes dry. Cook about 30 minutes in all. Sauce should be thick when done. On removing from fire, mix in:

$\frac{1}{2}$ cup lemon juice

3 tablespoons chicken broth

Let stand a few minutes before serving.

SERVE Chicken in portions on serving platter, with sauce over it.

Chicken with Almonds
Tsfaia

STEP 1 Cook the following together in covered casserole over medium fire until chicken is done:

1 medium-sized chicken

$\frac{1}{4}$ cup onion, diced

$\frac{1}{4}$ teaspoon ginger

$\frac{1}{2}$ teaspoon black pepper

$\frac{1}{4}$ teaspoon saffron

1 teaspoon salt

1 cup butter (or olive oil)

2 cups water

1 cup raw almonds (blanched and peeled) or 1 cup chickpeas which have soaked in water overnight

If stock goes dry, add a little *hot* water.

STEP 2 When chicken is cooked, remove it from casserole, and add into casserole:

1 large sweet white onion, sliced in rings

$\frac{1}{2}$ cup parsley, minced

1 tiny sprig fresh cardamon, if available

Continue cooking until onion is tender. Do not stir or otherwise crush onion. If chicken needs reheating before serving, return it to sauce for a few minutes.

SERVE Hot, on platter, with almond-onion sauce over it.

Chicken with Eggs and Almonds
Sjdeda Bilbeid Bilooz

STEP 1 Clean and cut up one or more chickens and bathe the portions in a mixture of:

2 tablespoons hot water
½ teaspoon saffron
½ teaspoon salt

STEP 2 Put in a deep pot, one after the other:

the chicken
1 cup onion, diced fine
1 teaspoon black pepper
1 heaped tablespoon cinnamon
½ teaspoon ground cumin seed
¼ teaspoon ginger
¼ teaspoon curry
¼ teaspoon grated nutmeg
½ cup parsley, chopped fine
1 scant tablespoon salt
⅓ cup olive oil (poured over all)
1 tablespoon butter

Cook over high fire, stirring contents frequently for 10 minutes. (Moroccans, holding lid on firmly with both hands, simply shake or toss the whole pot in the air.) Then add:

4 cups hot water (if a very large chicken or 2 chickens, add an extra cup water)

Cover and continue cooking until chicken is done (approx. 1 hour).

STEP 3 Apart, blanch and toast:
1 cup almonds

Apart also, hardboil:
1 egg per person

SERVE Chicken on individual plates, thus:
1 portion chicken (without sauce)
2 tablespoons almonds, as garnish
1 hardboiled egg, whole or quartered

Dress with:
1 tablespoon chicken stock

Note The sauce remaining from this and other similarly prepared chicken dishes makes a wonderful soup stock base for later use.

Chicken with Almonds and Cheese
Sjdeda Bi Looz Bi Shjbn

STEP 1 Put in deep pot or casserole:
    1 chicken, cut in portions
    1 cup onion, diced coarsely
    ½ cup parsley, minced
    1 teaspoon black pepper
    ¼ teaspoon saffron
    1 tablespoon cinnamon
    1 tablespoon salt
    ¼ teaspoon nutmeg
    ¼ teaspoon curry
    ¼ teaspoon ginger
    1 tablespoon butter
    4 cups warm water
Cover and cook over medium-high fire. When chicken is tender, remove from broth. Save broth for soup stock.

STEP 2 Add together in saucepan:
    7 tablespoons butter
    ¾ cup grated Parmesan
    1 tablespoon minced parsley
    ½ cup blanched, peeled, very lightly toasted almonds, chopped fine
Heat above almost to a boil, then add:
    1½ cups water (or chicken stock)
Mix well, then over a low flame bathe chicken in sauce until it is golden and has absorbed much of liquid.
SERVE Hot, with any remaining sauce as dressing.

Chicken with Olives and Lemon
M'Kuli

STEP 1 Add together:
    1 cup onion, minced

¼ teaspoon ginger
¼ teaspoon saffron
1 clove garlic, minced
1 teaspoon salt
1 cup olive oil
2 cups warm water

Without putting on fire, stir the above together until it is creamy.

STEP 2   Heat blended ingredients of Step 1 in casserole, and lay chicken in the liquid. Cover with lid and let cook over medium-high fire. Check and baste occasionally until done. Add *hot* water if needed.

STEP 3   *Optional:* With this as with other chicken recipes the Fezzi usually add vegetables when chicken is almost done, so that vegetable flavours are heightened by cooking in stock. The vegetables most often used are green beans, carrots and artichokes.

SERVE   Chicken on serving platter, with any vegetables alongside. Ladle over it all several tablespoons of stock sauce. Garnish with:

1 cup olives
1 conserved lemon rind, diced

Olives and lemon in this recipe will not have been cooked. If using prepared, salty olives, allow to soak in water first for ½ hour to remove excess salt.

Note The use of chicken livers in all Moroccan chicken *tadjeens* is important. When the chicken is removed, the liver, crushed into a paste in the stock, helps thicken and flavour the sauce.

Chicken with Lemon and Olives
M'Kuli

This recipe may also be applied successfully to meat, preferably lamb or mutton.

Put into pot:

the chicken (or meat)
¼ teaspoon ginger
1 teaspoon powdered cumin seed

2 tiny hot red peppers
salt to taste
1 cup olive oil
2 cups water

Cover and cook over a medium-high fire for ½ hour; then add the following which has been crushed together in the mortar:

1 cup onion, diced
½ cup parsley, cut up fine
1 clove garlic (optional)
1 small sprig fresh cardamon (if available)

Continue cooking until meat is tender. If vegetables are to be served, add them in about 20 minutes before chicken should be done. Five minutes before removing from fire, add into casserole:

½ cup olives (which have soaked in water ¼ hour to remove excess salt)
¼ cup lemon juice

SERVE Hot, with olives scattered over top, and dressed with remaining sauce.

Chicken with Olives and Lemon
Sjej bi Zaytoon Bi Lemoon

STEP 1 Put altogether in casserole:

1 chicken, cut up in serving portions
½ cup onion, chopped fine
1 cup parsley, chopped fine
½ teaspoon black pepper
¼ teaspoon ginger
1 teaspoon cinnamon (optional)
¼ teaspoon saffron
1 tablespoon salt
1 cup olive oil
2 tablespoons butter

Cook over high fire for 10 minutes, stirring constantly, until golden brown. Then add:

4–5 cups boiling water

Cover and continue cooking. Add more water only if pot goes dry.

STEP 2 When chicken is all but cooked and tender, add in:

1 whole preserved lemon (or 2 preserved limes) including rind, diced fine

1 cup green olives (which have soaked in water ¼ hour to remove excess salt)

Continue cooking chicken for another 10 minutes. If desired, broth may be thickened just before removing from fire with a light flour-water mixture.

SERVE   Hot with sauce ladled over meat.

Chicken with Olives and Lime
Sjdeda Bi Zatoon Bi Lima

STEP 1   Pound into a paste in the mortar:

8 cloves garlic, peeled

1 sprig fresh cardamon (if available)

½ tablespoon coarse salt

½ teaspoon saffron

Rub paste inside of and all over chicken. Tuck chicken legs into cavity. Put in wide casserole:

the chicken

¾ cup olive oil (pour over fowl)

⅓ cup butter (or margarine)

Clamp lid on tight and set over medium-high fire. After 10 minutes, add:

4–5 cups hot water (enough to cover chicken)

Turn chicken over after ½ hour, check for tenderness. Turn and stir occasionally, always replacing lid. Add more (hot) water if pot goes dry.

STEP 2   When chicken is done (about 1¼ hours) and just before removing from fire, toss into pot with chicken:

½ cup green olives

the rind of 2 preserved limes, diced fine

(Both olives and limes must be soaked in water, separately, for ¼ hour or so to remove excess salt, before use.)

SERVE   Hot on large serving platter, garnished with the olives and lemon, and sauce ladled over.

Chicken with Pumpkin
Jedj Ul Garagh Hamarah

STEP 1 Add together:
    1 cup onion, minced
    ¼ teaspoon ginger
    ¼ teaspoon saffron
    1 clove garlic, minced
    ½ teaspoon salt
    1 cup olive oil
    2 cups water

Without putting over fire, stir and blend the above until it is creamy.

STEP 2 Heat ingredients of Step 1 in casserole for five minutes over high fire, then lay chicken in liquid. Cover and cook over medium fire. Check and baste occasionally. If necessary to add water, make sure it is hot.

STEP 3 Apart, cut up pumpkin in chunks and fry in oil until soft. Remove pumpkin from frying pan and mash; mix into it:
    cinnamon, to taste
    sugar, to taste

The pumpkin should be rather sweet. Remove *most* of the oil from frying pan, and return purée to pan. Cook, stirring until a nice brown colour.

SERVE Hot, with pumpkin purée accompanying chicken in the same manner as potato purée, *or*, serve pumpkin as sauce.

Chicken with Raisins
Sjdeda Sbeeb Ubsaal

STEP 1 Put all together in casserole:
    chicken, cut in serving portions
    ½ cup onion, diced fine
    ½ teaspoon black pepper
    1 teaspoon cinnamon
    ¼ teaspoon ginger
    ¼ teaspoon nutmeg
    1 tablespoon salt

½ cup parsley, cut up fine
½ cup olive oil
½ cup butter

Cook over high fire, stirring, for 10 minutes.
Then add:

5 cups very hot water

Cover tightly with lid and continue cooking.

STEP 2 When chicken is three-quarters cooked, add in:
2 cups raisins
2 cups onion, sliced thin lengthwise

SERVE Hot, when both chicken and onion are cooked.

Chicken with Rice
Sjedj Bi Rooza

STEP 1 Cook together in casserole until chicken is done:
chicken
½ cup onion, diced
¼ teaspoon ginger
1 bay leaf
½ teaspoon black pepper
¼ teaspoon saffron
1 teaspoon salt
1 cup olive oil
2 cups water

Add hot water if liquid cooks off.

STEP 2 Wash 1 to 2 cups uncooked rice and tie it up in a piece of
clean fine gauze (allowing room for rice to expand). Twenty
minutes before chicken is to be done, place this along
with chicken in broth; rice then takes the flavour of the
chicken.

SERVE Hot, with drops of lemon juice over all.

Chicken with Rice and Lemon
Sjdeda Birooz bi Lemoon

STEP 1 Put together in casserole:

1 chicken, cut in serving portions
½ cup onion, diced fine
½ cup parsley, cut up fine
1 teaspoon black pepper
1 teaspoon cinnamon
¼ teaspoon nutmeg
¼ teaspoon saffron
¼ teaspoon curry
¼ teaspoon ginger
1 tablespoon salt
¾ cup olive oil

Bring to a golden colour over a high fire, stirring frequently, for 10 minutes. Then add:

4 cups boiling hot water

Lower fire, cover and let simmer until tender.

STEP 2 Apart, hardboil:

1 egg for each person

STEP 3 Apart, put together in a saucepan:

1 quart water
2 teaspoons salt
2 tablespoons parsley, cut up fine
¼ teaspoon saffron

Bring the above to a boil, then add:

1½ cups rice.

When rice is cooked, drain.

SERVE   On individual plates thus: 1 chicken portion (without sauce), 1 rice portion, 2 tablespoons stock over all. Garnish with hardboiled eggs, quartered. Squeeze a few drops of lemon over all.

Roast Chicken with Almond Carrot Stuffing

Sjdeda M'Haamarh

STEP 1 Bathe chicken with a blend of:

¼ teaspoon saffron
1 teaspoon salt
¼ cup hot water

STEP 2 For the stuffing boil together in water until tender:

2 cups carrots, finely cubed

1 cup onion, diced

1 tablespoon salt

½ cup parsley, chopped fine

Drain carrots when cooked, and add to them:

½ cup blanched, peeled, toasted almonds, ground up

1 teaspoon black pepper

1 teaspoon salt

¼ cup butter

1 teaspoon cinnamon

Blend stuffing ingredients thoroughly. Stuff chicken with this mixture and truss.

STEP 3 Melt on shallow roasting platter

¼ cup butter

Place chicken on platter. If any stuffing is left over, distribute it around on platter to make sauce. Put in hot preheated oven. After 10 minutes, lower heat to medium, at the same time adding ½ cup water. Check frequently and turn chicken over when golden on one side. Be sure to prick with fork so that juices run out. Baste often; do not cover.

Variation: Ground peanuts may be used in place of almonds in the stuffing.

Alternative Stuffing – for Chicken or Turkey. Mix together:

½ cup blanched, peeled and slightly toasted almonds, chopped fine

1 cup raisins (which have been soaked 1 hour, or boiled 10 minutes)

2 cups bread crumbs

1 egg

1 teaspoon salt

½ teaspoon cinnamon

½ teaspoon ginger

½ teaspoon pepper

Chicken (or Meat) Stew
Tajine Sweri

STEP 1 Cook chicken or meat (preferably lamb or mutton) following the same procedure as Step 1 of Bastela (see p. 49). When meat is removed from sauce (and boned in the case of chicken), place it in an oven-baking dish which may also be used for serving.

STEP 2 Continue cooking stock until only oil-vegetable mixture remains. Remove from fire and stir into hot oil mixture:
10 raw broken eggs

Mix well and when egg white begins to show that it is slightly cooked, pour sauce over meat, and finish all in preheated oven.

SERVE Hot, in baking dish. Lemon drops may be added.

Chicken Barbecue
Sjdeda Mischui

STEP 1 Pound into a paste in the mortar:
½ cup onion, diced fine
½ cup parsley, minced
1 tablespoon salt
1 teaspoon black pepper

Rub paste over surface of chicken and dot it with butter. Put some spice paste and 1 tablespoon butter inside cavity.

STEP 2 Spit chicken on stick or wire skewer and roast barbecue-style over a good smokeless wood fire or hot charcoals. Turn slowly and often, and do not allow fire to touch fowl. Prick skin and muscles with a fork. Baste with butter and spice paste frequently and whenever skin shows signs of drying.

SERVE Hot, when tender and golden brown.

Turkey (or Chicken) Stuffed with Couscous (or rice)
Bibi M'Ahmarh

STEP 1 Steam couscous in colander over boiling water for 20 minutes until grains are soft but still firm. If using rice, *half* cook it in standard procedure.

STEP 2 For the stuffing blend together:
the steamed couscous (or rice)

1 cup seedless raisins (which have soaked in water for a
    few minutes)
1 teaspoon cinnamon
¼ teaspoon nutmeg
½ teaspoon salt
2 tablespoons sugar (or vary to taste)
2 tablespoons butter

After blending the above well together, butter the inside of fowl,
then pack the stuffing in firmly up to the neck, and truss.

STEP 3 Put into casserole:
    ½ cup onion, diced
    1 clove garlic, diced
    2 hot red chili peppers
    ¼ teaspoon ginger
    1 teaspoon salt
    1¾ cup olive oil
    3 cups water

Allow to cook for 10–15 minutes, then lay fowl in casserole, cover
with lid and continue cooking. Add (hot) water only if pot goes
dry. When turkey or chicken is cooked and tender, remove from
casserole. Add into the boiling stock, to make sauce:
    2 tablespoons couscous (or rice)
Continue cooking stock until couscous or rice is done.

SERVE   Chicken on serving platter, with sauce laid over it. Drops
        of lemon juice may be added.

Doves
Lekleeya Dzireeya

This is a North African dish of Algerian origin, for feast days.
Pigeon or squab may be used instead of doves, and one fowl should
be allowed for each person. Ingredients given here are adequate
for preparing 5–7 doves.

STEP 1 Put together in deep casserole:
    the doves (whole or halved)
    ½ head garlic, peeled
    ½ cup parsley, minced
    1 teaspoon black pepper

            1 tablespoon salt
            ¼ teaspoon saffron
            ½ cup olive oil
Cook over high fire, turning constantly for 5 to 10 minutes. Then lower heat and add:
            1 quart hot water
Cover and continue cooking until tender. Remove doves from broth, bone and cut meat up in very small pieces.

STEP 2 Add together in saucepan:
            1 cup onion, minced
            1 cup parsley, minced
            ½ cup butter
            2 cups tomatoes, mashed or cubed fine
            ¼ cup water
            ½ teaspoon salt
            the dove meat
Simmer together until ingredients are well blended and tomato and onion are cooked.

STEP 3 When cooked, break in carefully on top of mixture, distributing one at a time around on top of dish:
            1 raw egg per person
            Allow eggs to poach.

SERVE   Hot, in same casserole, with a few drops of lemon juice squeezed over all.

Steamed Chicken
Sjdeda M'Fourh

Bathe chicken in mixture of:
            1 tablespoon salt
            ½ teaspoon saffron
            3 tablespoons hot water
Place chicken in a colander or other container with perforated bottom, and set it over a pot of boiling water. Cover chicken with thick cloth and allow it to steam for about 1½ hours, or until tender. When done, chicken may be bathed in butter and spices, according to individual tastes.

SERVE   Hot – or cold in salad.

MEATS

Lamb with Prunes

STEP 1 Cut the leg of lamb in portions and put it in casserole. Add in over the meat:

- 1 medium-sized onion, cut up
- 1 small handful of parsley and chervil
- 2 teaspoons salt
- $\frac{1}{4}$ teaspoon nutmeg
- $\frac{1}{4}$ teaspoon ginger
- $\frac{1}{4}$ teaspoon curry
- $\frac{1}{4}$ teaspoon saffron
- $\frac{1}{4}$ teaspoon black pepper
- 1 tablespoon butter
- $\frac{1}{2}$ cup oil (pour over all)

Cook over medium-high fire for 10–15 minutes, turning over the meat constantly. Then add:

- 4 cups hot water

Continue cooking about $1\frac{1}{2}$ hours until meat is done.

STEP 2 Apart, boil in water until they are cooked but still firm:

- 1 lb prunes

Drain, then sprinkle with:

- 2 tablespoons sugar
- 2 teaspoons cinnamon

Gently shake prunes around until well mixed with sugar and cinnamon.

SERVE Meat on platter with prunes tossed over it.

Tongue with Almonds
L'Sen M'Tayeeb Bi Looz

STEP 1 Put together in casserole:

- 1 tongue (veal or lamb)
- 6 stalks parsley

    1 large onion, quartered
    1 teaspoon black pepper
    2 tablespoons salt
    cold water to cover

Place lid on and cook over medium-high fire. When tongue is cooked and tender (2 to 3 hours for veal, 1½ for lamb), remove from fire. Drain. Plunge immediately into cold water; remove skin and slice.

STEP 2 Preheat in saucepan:
    ¼ cup oil

Add to hot (not boiling) oil:
    1 cup onion, diced very fine
    ½ cup parsley, minced
    1 teaspoon ground cumin seed
    1 teaspoon black pepper
    1 scant tablespoon salt

Cook 2–3 minutes, stirring. Then add:
    2 cups water
    1 tablespoon paprika (or ¼ teaspoon saffron)
    ½ cup blanched, raw almonds, ground or chopped fine

STEP 3 When sauce (Step 2) boils, add in tongue slices and simmer over slow fire for 25–30 minutes. The longer it is cooked, the better it is. It also improves with reheating.

SERVE Hot, with sauce, and drops of lemon juice added.

Liver with Olives

Tadjeen L'Kibda

(Serves 3)

STEP 1 Heat to a simmer in casserole:
    ½ cup oil

Then add, one after the other over fire, stirring:
    ½ tablespoon sweet red pepper
    2 cloves garlic, chopped fine
    ½ teaspoon hot red peppers
    1 tablespoon salt
    1 lb liver, cut in bite-size pieces (beef, veal or calf can be used)

½ cup parsley, chopped fine
2 cups warm water
Cover and cook over high fire for about 20 minutes.

STEP 2 After 20 minutes add:
    1 cup prepared black olives
Lower heat and cook 10 minutes more.

SERVE   Hot, with drops of lemon juice squeezed over each serving. (Remember that if green olives are used, they must be put in boiling water first for 5–10 minutes to remove excess salt.)

Meatball-Tomato Stew
L'Kifta Bi Stumatish
(Serves 4)

STEP 1 Shape into 1″ meatballs and put aside:
    1 lb ground beef or veal (rump, round of chuck roast)
(Moistening hands with water aids this operation.)

STEP 2 Warm up in frying pan or saucepan:
    ½ cup oil
Then add quickly, one by one to the oil over fire:
    1 tablespoon sweet red pepper
    1 head garlic, peeled and chopped fine
    1 teaspoon hot red peppers, chopped up
    1 heaped teaspoon ground cumin seed
    1 heaped teaspoon salt
    2 cups whole tomatoes
    ½ cup parsley, chopped fine
    1 cup warm water
Bring ingredients to a boil, stir well and let boil for 5 minutes; then add meatballs and continue cooking 15–20 minutes more.

STEP 3 Break in, one at a time, placing them around the sides of pan:
    4 raw eggs
Remove from fire and serve when eggs are poached.

Tripe (1)

L'Daowah

(Serves 4)

STEP 1 Add together in casserole:

    1½ lbs tripe, well washed in salt water, and cut up in bite-
    size pieces

    ½ cup parsley, minced

    1 head garlic, peeled and chopped very fine

    1½ tablespoons sweet red pepper (paprika)

    1 tablespoon ground cumin seed

    1 tablespoon salt

    ½ teaspoon hot red peppers, cut up fine

    ½ cup olive oil

    8 cups cold water

Cover and cook over medium-high fire for about 2 hours. Add
more water if needed.

STEP 2 When tripe is nearly done, add:

    3 cups tomatoes, mashed

    6 whole peeled potatoes

SERVE Hot, when potatoes are done.

Variation: Dried beans are often added in Step 2 instead of
potatoes. This calls for more water.

Tripe (2)

L'Daowah

STEP 1 Add together in casserole:

    1½ lbs tripe, well washed in salty water, and cut up in small
    pieces

    1 tablespoon salt

    1 cup onion, cubed

    ½ teaspoon hot red peppers, cut up fine

    8 cups cold water

    ½ cup oil

Cover and cook over medium-high fire for 2 hours, or more,
depending on quality. Add more water if needed.

STEP 2 When all but done add in:

$\frac{1}{2}$ cup light vinegar
1 teaspoon ground cumin seed

SERVE   Hot or cooled, with drops of lemon juice and a garnish of minced parsley.

Braised Shoulder of Lamb
Mischui

STEP 1   Cook together in covered casserole on stove until meat is *almost* well done:
shoulder of lamb
1 medium-sized onion, cut up
2 cloves garlic
salt to taste
very little water

STEP 2   Apart, crush together in mortar:
$\frac{1}{4}$ cup mint leaves, cut up
2 teaspoons ground cumin seed
3 tiny red hot chili peppers

STEP 3   Remove lamb meat from pot. Add ingredients of Step 2 into remaining onion-garlic-meat stock, blending well. Place meat in oven-serving dish. Pour sauce over it, and finish in the oven, basting well.

SERVE   Hot, in oven-serving dish.

Hamburger Stew
F'Tadjeen L'Kifta
(Serves 5)

STEP 1   Make meatballs 1″ thick with:
1 lb finely ground beef or veal
Allow to stand awhile.

STEP 2   Place one atop the other in layers in casserole:
meatballs
2 cups potatoes, peeled, cubed coarsely
$\frac{1}{2}$ cup onion, sliced fine lengthwise
$\frac{1}{2}$ cup tomato, crushed
$\frac{1}{2}$ cup parsley, minced

1 teaspoon sweet red pepper
1 teaspoon black pepper
1 tablespoon salt
¼ teaspoon saffron
2 cups water
½ cup oil (or equivalent in suet)

Cover and cook over high fire. Mix after 10 minutes, lower fire and continue cooking. Check occasionally. Stew is ready to serve when potatoes and meat are both cooked.

Leg of Lamb or Mutton (1)
Rzhla del Ranmee

STEP 1 Cut through the meat and bones of leg in several places.

STEP 2 Pound into a paste in the mortar:

   2 stalks mint, cut up
   2 stalks cardamon, cut up (if available)
   6 stalks parsley, cut up
   6 cloves garlic, peeled
   1 small onion, cut up
   1 tablespoon salt

Add in, mixing well:

   1 teaspoon cumin seed, ground
   1 teaspoon black pepper
   1 heaped tablespoon sweet red pepper

Rub the spice paste generously all over and into the meat.

STEP 3 Put the meat in a casserole wide enough to allow meat to lie flat as possible. Pour over it:

   1¾ cups olive oil

Set on high fire with lid on tight. In 5 minutes, check, turn over and mix around. Five minutes later, add:

   2 quarts hot water (or enough to half cover the meat)

Keep casserole tightly covered; check meat occasionally. After an hour of cooking turn meat over. In 1½ hours, liquid may have cooked almost off. Add 1-2 cups water. When liquid has again boiled done (about 2 hours) meat should be ready.

SERVE Hot on large serving platter with any remaining stock as sauce.

Leg of Lamb or Mutton Pot Roast (2)
Rzhla del Ranmee

STEP 1 Plunge knife into the leg of lamb (approx. 5 lbs of meat), in half a dozen places and insert 1 peeled clove of garlic at each point, pushing it well into the meat.

STEP 2 Rub over the meat a mixture of:
3 tablespoons butter
2 teaspoons salt
2 teaspoons crushed cumin seed
1 teaspoon black pepper

STEP 3 Warm up in roasting pan:
½ cup oil

Lay meat in pan, cover and set over medium fire. Check carefully, turning when browned. After 20 minutes, or before if pot goes dry, add in:
¼ cup butter

SERVE With parsley garnish and drops of lemon.

Meat with Almond Sauce
Maha'dahr Tadjeen Bi Looz
(Serves 6)

STEP 1 Put in casserole together:
2¼ lbs stew meat, cut in portions (may be chuck or round of beef, leg or shoulder of mutton or lamb)
2 cups onion, diced fine
¼ teaspoon saffron
½ teaspoon black pepper
1 heaped teaspoon *lacama* (see p. 65)
1 tablespoon salt
½ teaspoon cinnamon
½ cup parsley, minced
rind of one orange or lemon (using only coloured part), cut in fine strips
1 cup olive oil (poured over all)

Cover and cook over medium-high fire, stirring frequently, for 15 minutes. Then add:
5 cups hot water

Re-cover, and continue cooking until meat is done.

STEP 2 Just before removing from fire, add in, mixing well with
the meat and remaining stock:

  1 cup blanched, peeled and toasted almonds, ground up or
    chopped; sprinkle almonds very lightly with salt before
    toasting.

If stew is too thick, a little water may be added.

SERVE Hot, immediately.

Brains
Mogh

STEP 1 Wash, then soak brains in cold salted water for $\frac{1}{2}$ hour.
Rinse, then drop in boiling water with a pinch of salt.
Leave boil about 10 minutes, until toughened and nearly
cooked. Drain, cool and slice in portions or cube.

STEP 2 Put in saucepan:

  2 cups tomatoes
  $\frac{1}{4}$ cup parsley, minced
  3 cloves garlic, minced
  $\frac{1}{2}$ cup onion, diced fine
  $\frac{1}{2}$ teaspoon ground cumin seed
  $\frac{1}{4}$ teaspoon black pepper
  $\frac{1}{4}$ teaspoon saffron
  1 teaspoon salt
  7 tablespoons butter (or $\frac{1}{4}$ cup oil)

Bring above to a simmer, then add:

  $\frac{1}{2}$ cup warm water

Continue cooking sauce for about 10 minutes.

STEP 3 Add brains to sauce over fire and allow to simmer until
brains have well absorbed the sauce, and the onion is
cooked. (Approx. 20 mins.)

SERVE Hot, garnished with minced parsley and drops of lemon.

Note One beef brain serves 3-4.   One lamb brain serves 2.

Liver Stew
L'Kibda Bitskulya
(Serves 4)

STEP 1 Wash and cut up in bite-size cubes:
   1 lb liver (can be veal, beef, calf, lamb or mutton but the latter two are the tenderest)

STEP 2 Heat to a simmer in saucepan or frying pan, but do not allow to burn or smoke:
   ¼ cup oil
Add, quickly, one after the other:
   1 tablespoon sweet red pepper
   ½ cup water
   ½ teaspoon hot red peppers
   ½ head garlic, peeled and diced fine
   ½ cup parsley, chopped fine
   1 heaped tablespoon salt
   1 teaspoon ground cumin seed
Bring to a boil, then add:
   1½ cups fresh tomatoes, cut up fine
When sauce boils again, add in:
   the liver
Cover and continue cooking for 20–25 minutes. Stir frequently, adding ¼ to ½ cup water as needed.

STEP 3 Just before removing from fire, break in one at a time and distribute around the pan:
   4 raw eggs

SERVE When eggs are poached, with a few drops of lemon over each serving.

Meatballs and Carrot Stew
L'Kifta Bi Ja'ada
(Serves 5)

STEP 1 Mould into meatballs and set aside:
   1 lb beef or veal, ground fine

STEP 2 Put all together in casserole:

1 cup onion, diced fine

$\frac{1}{2}$ cup parsley, chopped fine

2 teaspoons cinnamon

1 teaspoon black pepper

$\frac{1}{4}$ teaspoon saffron

1 tablespoon salt

$\frac{1}{2}$ cup oil

Cover and cook over high fire for about 10 minutes, stirring frequently. Then add:

3 cups water

Bring liquid to a boil and allow to boil for five minutes; then add in:

the meatballs

Leave simmer about 20 minutes more.

STEP 3 Apart, put in another saucepan:

4 cups carrots, diced medium fine

1 teaspoon salt

water to cover

Cook until tender, then drain.

STEP 4 Add carrots to meat stew. If stew has already finished cooking, reheat to boiling point.

SERVE Hot – with those important few drops of lemon juice.

Kidneys with Sauce

L'Kleowee

(Serves 3)

STEP 1 Put in casserole over the fire, one by one:

$\frac{1}{2}$ cup oil

1 lb kidneys, sliced (may be calf, beef, veal or lamb)

1 teaspoon black pepper

4 cloves garlic, diced fine

$\frac{1}{2}$ cup parsley, minced

$\frac{1}{4}$ teaspoon saffron

1 laurel or bay leaf

1 tablespoon salt

Cook for 10 minutes, stirring constantly. Then add:

$1\frac{1}{2}$ cups warm water

4

Cover and continue cooking over high fire for 30 minutes. Add more water if needed. If desired, sauce may be thickened slightly with flour at the last minute.

SERVE   Potatoes go well with this dish which should be served hot, with lemon juice squeezed over.

Variation Although Moslems are forbidden wine and do not use it in cookery, I find that a cup of white wine substituted for the water, makes this dish even better.

Mutton–Carrot Stew
L'Ha'am de Runwee F'Tadjeen
(Serves 5)

The leg, shoulder, shank, saddle or crown roasts of mutton are tasty made according to this recipe. Have the butcher crack the bones, but otherwise leave the meat in one piece.

STEP 1   Put together in deep casserole over a high fire:

> 2¼ lbs mutton
> 1 cup onion, diced
> ½ cup parsley, chopped very fine
> 1 teaspoon black pepper
> ½ teaspoon cinnamon
> ¼ teaspoon saffron
> 1 tablespoon salt
> ½ cup olive oil

Cover and cook, stirring frequently, for 10 minutes – until meat has pretty well absorbed the oil. Then add:

> 4 cups hot water

Continue cooking until the meat is three-quarters done (about 45 mins.), depending on quality.

STEP 2   When meat is nearly done, add:

> 4 cups carrots, diced

Continue cooking, but now remove lid so that evaporation takes place. Meat is ready to serve when carrots are done.

SERVE   Hot, with a spoonful of sauce; garnish with carrots and a few drops of lemon.

Meat with Olives and Lemon
L'Ha'am Bi Zaytoon Bi Lemoon

Leg or shoulder of lamb are tastiest in this dish, but mutton or beef may also be used successfully.

STEP 1 Lay one ingredient in atop the other in this order:
2½ lbs meat
1 tablespoon salt
6 stalks parsley
½ teaspoon black pepper
1 teaspoon *lacama* (equal portions of cinnamon, nutmeg, ginger, curry, black pepper)
¼ teaspoon powdered saffron
1 cup diced onion
½ cup olive oil

Braise, watching closely and stirring often for 15 minutes. Then add:
1 cup hot water
Cover tightly and cook until meat is tender.

STEP 2 Apart, boil for 10 minutes to remove excess salt:
1½ cups green olives
Drain olives and add them to the meat when meat is nearly done. At the same time, add in:
the yellow part (only) of the rind of 1 lemon, finely diced. Use preserved lemon rind if on hand.

SERVE Hot on serving platter, garnished with lemon and olives, and dressed with a little sauce.

Lamb with Onion Dressing
Camama

Camama is a favourite Moroccan dish, and one of the best known.

STEP 1 Cook together in covered casserole:
4–5 lbs lamb (or mutton)
¼ cup onion, diced
1 tablespoon cinnamon (or more)
¼ teaspoon ginger
¼ teaspoon nutmeg

1 teaspoon salt
3 to 4 tablespoons honey (or sugar)
1 cup olive oil
2 cups water

When meat is *half-cooked*, remove it from casserole and place it in an oven-casserole in which it will be served.

STEP 2 Spread over the meat and entire dish, lots and lots of onion rings (sweet white onion), in a thick layer. Pour over it a little of the meat stock-sauce. Put oven-casserole in preheated oven, but keep heat low so that onions brown nicely. Add sauce frequently and keep basting until meat is done. Onions should become very brown.

SERVE Hot, with onion dressing layed thickly over the meat.

Kidney Stew
Kleowee F'Tadjeen

STEP 1 Heat (but do not boil) in casserole:
¼ cup oil

Fry sliced kidneys very slightly in oil, but do not brown them. Remove kidneys from oil and put in oil:
½ cup finely diced onion

Leave onion till slightly golden, then add in:
the kidneys
¼ cup parsley, chopped fine
1½ teaspoons salt
1 teaspoon black pepper
bay leaf
½ cup tomato, finely cubed

Stir constantly, cooking over medium fire, until ingredients become like a smooth sauce. Then add:
½ cup warm water

STEP 2 When ingredients are just about to boil, add in:
1 cup potato, cubed
1 cup carrots, cubed

SERVE Hot, when potatoes are done.

Honey Roast

L'Ha'am Ma'assel

(Serves 6)

Mutton, veal, beef or lamb may be used here. Shoulder, shank, saddle roast or any inexpensive cut is surprisingly good prepared in this way. Bones included with meat lend extra flavour.

STEP 1 Put together in casserole:

    2¼ lbs meat, cut in chunky portions

    1 cup onion diced

    1 cup parsley, minced

    ½ teaspoon ginger

    ½ teaspoon curry

    ½ teaspoon nutmeg

    2 teaspoons black pepper

    1 tablespoon salt

    1 tablespoon cinnamon

    ¼ teaspoon saffron

    1 cup oil

Cover and cook over high fire for 10–15 minutes, stirring frequently – until meat is browned and has absorbed most of the oil and spices. Then add:

    5 cups hot water

Continue cooking, with lid on, until meat is tender (approx. 30 mins. for lamb, 1 hour for other meats). Add more (hot) water if needed.

STEP 2 When meat is cooked and tender, mix together:

    ½ cup honey (or 1 scant cup sugar)

    1 tablespoon cinnamon

Add sugar and cinnamon to roast and mix well.

Continue cooking meat until liquid reaches the consistency of light oil (or when if sugar is used, it has melted) – about 10 minutes. The colour of the meat will be dark.

SERVE   On individual plates with meat sauce. For a special treat garnish with a sprinkling of ground almonds, which have been blanched, peeled and lightly toasted.

Roast Lamb (or Mutton) with Quince
L'Ha'am Sfarjehl Ma'asel
(Serves 6)

This is a favourite Moroccan dish. Inexpensive cuts can be employed with success, and the recipe may also be applied to beef, using rump or round roast.

STEP 1 Put together in deep casserole:
>   2¼ lbs of meat, cut in portions
>   ½ cup onion, diced fine
>   ¼ teaspoon saffron
>   1 heaped teaspoon *lacama* (equal proportions: cinnamon, curry, ginger, black pepper, nutmeg)
>   1 tablespoon salt
>   ½ cup parsley, minced
>   1 cup oil

Cover and cook over high fire, stirring frequently for 10 minutes, when meat will have pretty well absorbed the spices and liquid. Then add:
>   5 cups hot water

Cover and continue cooking until meat is done.

STEP 2 Apart, peel, core and quarter:
>   6–7 quinces

Score a cross on the outside of each quarter. Boil quinces in two quarts of water until cooked but still firm, then drain.

STEP 3 Make a light syrup by bringing once to a boil:
>   1 cup sugar
>   2 cups water

Then add to the syrup:
>   the quinces
>   1 tablespoon cinnamon

Bring syrup with quinces once again to a boil, then remove from fire.

SERVE   Directly on plates when meat is cooked: meat portion first, garnished with 3 or 4 pieces of quince. Dress with a spoonful of sauce from the meat, then a bit of the quince syrup over all.

Variation Very tart apples are sometimes used instead of quinces.

SALADS

Carrot Salad
Schlada Dsjada
(Serves 6)

This is a unique salad and worth trying. It goes very well with fish.

STEP 1 Boil together:
   1 quart water
   3 cups carrots, sliced crosswise
   1 teaspoon salt

Remove from fire when carrots are tender but still slightly under-cooked. Set aside *in their water* to cool.

STEP 2 Pound into a paste in mortar:
   5 cloves garlic, peeled
   ¼ cup parsley, minced
   ½ teaspoon hot red peppers
   1 tablespoon sweet red pepper
   1 teaspoon salt
   1 teaspoon ground cumin seed

STEP 3 Heat in frying pan or saucepan:
   ¼ cup oil

Add in, mixing:
   the spice paste (Step 2)
   1 cup water from carrots

When liquid boils, remove from fire and add it to carrots and their stock. Then add:
   ½ cup lemon juice (or light vinegar)

SERVE Cold, today, tomorrow or later. Kept cool and covered, carrot salad, preserved by spices, will keep for a week.

Riffi County Salad
Schlada Fikteeb

For this barbecued country salad, have a smokeless charcoal or, preferably, wood fire. The following, which provides for one serving, would be multiplied by the numbers of persons.

STEP 1 Cut in quarters, lengthwise:

    1 tomato

    1 fresh green pepper

    1 onion

Spit a section of each vegetable alternately with one of another on a skewer, and salt. Roast over fire barbecue-style (or with skewers resting on edges of a roasting pan, in the oven).

SERVE Remove from skewers onto serving plate; squeeze lemon juice over salad.

Baked Salad
Schlada Mischuia
(Serves 6)

STEP 1 Place 5–6 firm ripe tomatoes and 7–8 fresh green peppers in oven and leave until skins of peppers and tomatoes are almost burnt. Then plunge them immediately in cold water. Remove skin of both peppers and tomatoes. Cube for salad in $\frac{1}{2}$" chunks.

STEP 2 For the dressing mix together:

    1 onion, minced

    2 heaped tablespoons minced parsley

    1 tablespoon salt

    2 tablespoons olive oil

    $\frac{1}{4}$ cup light vinegar – or juice of 2 lemons

Add dressing to peppers and tomatoes. All salads are best if allowed to marinate about 20 minutes before serving.

Cooked Salad
Schlada Mtayeebah bi Filfil
(Serves 4)

Warm up in deep frying pan:

    1 cup oil

Add:

      3 onions, quartered lengthwise

      5 tomatoes, skinned and crushed

      6 fresh green peppers, cut in lengthwise strips

      $\frac{1}{2}$ teaspoon hot red peppers

      $\frac{1}{2}$ teaspoon ground cumin seed

      1 teaspoon salt

      1 cup water

When mixture boils add:

      1 cup water

Continue cooking until onion is tender – about 15 mins.

SERVE Hot or cold.

Green Pepper Salad
Schlada L'Filfil

STEP 1 Plunge into boiling water:

      6 fresh green peppers (sweet)

      6 large, firm tomatoes

Remove tomatoes after 2–3 minutes. Leave peppers for 6–7 minutes longer. Chill both immediately in cold water.

Skin tomatoes and cut up in $\frac{1}{2}''$ squares. Skin peppers, remove seeds and core; cut each up in 6–8 lengthwise strips. Put both in salad bowl.

STEP 2 For the dressing add together in the following order:

      $\frac{1}{2}$ head garlic, peeled and minced

      1 teaspoon ground cumin seed

      $\frac{1}{4}$ teaspoon hot red peppers, cut up fine

      1 teaspoon salt

      5 tablespoons oil

      $\frac{1}{4}$ cup lemon juice or light vinegar

Pour dressing over peppers and tomatoes.

Leave to marinate 20 minutes before serving.

Relish Salad
Schlada L'Filfil

The Tetuani table is set at all times with this finely diced, almost minced salad, which serves also as a relish and is a splendid light accompaniment to heavy meat dishes.

Mix together:

    2 cucumbers, finely diced in $\frac{1}{4}$" or smaller cubes

    1 large firm tomato, finely diced in $\frac{1}{4}$" or smaller cubes

    1 medium-sized onion, finely diced in $\frac{1}{4}$" or smaller cubes

    2 hot red chili peppers, cut up fine (optional)

Dress with salt, oil and vinegar. Let marinate $\frac{1}{2}$ hour before serving.

VEGETABLE DISHES
✕ᑫᑯᑫᑲᑯᑲ✕

Tadjeen Gnaoua
(The vegetable stew of the Berber Negro Musicians)

The people of the unorthodox Gnaoua sect are negro, and among them, it is said, there are many saints. The true Gnaoua, whatever his degree of colour or saintliness, is always a musician – and thus 'Gnaoua' has come to denote a kind of music rather than the religious sect.

The Gnaoua are almost always poor, materially speaking, so that they are often vegetarians by force of circumstances – hence, the vegetable stew.

When they play their music and dance they believe their hearts to be pure and transparent. Transported by the music, which is repetitive and pulsating, to a state of ecstasy, they are gifted with mystic powers which are further enchanced by the exchange of coins. Whoever finds himself among them at such a time wanting to know the future needs only to ask.

On festive occasions the Gnaouas' knee-length, blouse-type dress is brilliant. One may wear a red tunic decorated in yellow, another green embroidered in red, another blue with orange. Though barefoot, all wear white turbans. As they sing and whirl about, the figures create a kaleidoscope of colour and action that mounts in intensity along with the song and the tempo of drums.

When the Sultan and independence returned to Morocco, every town celebrated in the streets. In Tangier, guilds marched in formation – the taxi drivers, the bank employees, the port workers, and all the rest. Here and there a man carried a child. Khaki-clad boy scout troops marched with soldierly dignity ahead of their bands of musicians; the lame and the blind who held hands in their halting progress drew applause; rich and poor, high and low, even a few women, they all bore themselves with a new pride.

And, there were the Gnaoua, dancing, not marching, down Rue Belgique, past the Café de Paris where tables were abruptly deserted for them. 'Tumpeta-tumpeta-tump-tump' – their primitive music sounded. The calloused black feet pranced the asphalt.

A clang of cymbals and tambourine, the thumping of the drum, and the contagious rhythm spread to the spectators, who demanded more and more and more. And the Gnaoua, who had been dancing since early morning, gave more, while the applause from the sidelines marked their progress on down the boulevard.

Here is how the Gnaoua make and flavour their vegetable stew.

STEP 1 Bring to a boil:
> 1 quart water
> 1 tablespoon salt

When water boils, add:
> 1 cup turnips, cubed
> 1 cup carrots, cubed
> 1 cup eggplant, cubed
> 1 cup potatoes, peeled and cubed
> 1 cup marrow, cubed
> 1 large onion, cubed
> 1 head garlic, peeled

Cook until vegetables are tender.

STEP 2 Preheat in frying pan:
> $\frac{1}{2}$ cup olive oil

Add to hot oil:
> $\frac{1}{2}$ tablespoon hot red peppers, chopped fine
> 1 teaspoon ground cumin seed
> 2 tablespoons parsley, chopped fine
> $\frac{1}{2}$ cup onion, diced fine

STEP 3 Add the vegetables and their stock to the ingredients in frying pan. The stew is ready when the onion is cooked.

Stuffed Squash or Marrow (1)

Ulkraa Kifta

(Serves 6)

STEP 1 Halve lengthwise and remove some of the pulp from:
> 6 small green marrows (large cucumber size)

STEP 2 Blend the following well together by hand:
> 1 teaspoon salt
> $\frac{1}{4}$ cup parsley, minced
> $\frac{1}{4}$ cup onion, minced

1 teaspoon sweet red pepper
1 teaspoon black pepper
1 lb finely ground veal or beef

STEP 3 Stuff the halves of squash or marrow. Fry in oil or butter –
or roast in broiler.

SERVE Hot with drops of lemon juice sprinkled over.

Stuffed Squash or Marrow (2)
Ulkraa Kifta
(For 6)

STEP 1 Cut off one end of each of 6 small green squashes (large
cucumber size) and hollow them out lengthwise.

STEP 2 Stuff with a mixture of:
1 lb finely ground veal or beef
a few grains of rice
a pinch of salt and pepper

STEP 3 Warm up in a large frying pan or saucepan:
$\frac{1}{4}$ cup oil

Add to heated oil, one by one, in this order:
1 teaspoon sweet red pepper
1 teaspoon salt
$\frac{1}{2}$ teaspoon black pepper
1 cup tomatoes cubed
$\frac{1}{2}$ cup onion diced
$\frac{1}{4}$ cup parsley

Stir and blend sauce well over the fire; then lay the stuffed marrow
into it. Turn them over frequently. Or, they may be baked in the
oven, in which case they may be turned over, or basted. Cooking
time is about $1\frac{1}{2}$ hours.

SERVE Hot, with drops of lemon juice.

Bean Purée

This dish, like many of the vegetable dishes, is eaten by the
hillsmen, for meat where they live is scarce, and only special
occasions call for the slaughter of an animal.

STEP 1 Bring nearly to a boil:
  1 quart water (unsalted)
Add:
  1 pint split broad beans
Boil beans until very tender. Drain, then crush beans into a paste and whip.

STEP 2 Add to the purée:
  2 pods hot red pepper
  4 cloves garlic, peeled and minced
  ½ teaspoon salt
  ½ teaspoon ground cumin seed
  2 tablespoons oil (or butter)

Lentils with Jerked Meat
L'Ahdoz bi Kadid

STEP 1 Boil together in water until tender:
  ¼ to ½ lb jerked meat (which if salted must first be soaked in water overnight)
  ½ lb lentils
  1 onion, quartered

STEP 2 Fry in heated oil until golden brown:
  2 large onions, sliced fine lengthwise
Then add:
  lentils and meat (Step 1)
  1 cup water
Simmer for ½ hour. Add water if needed; salt and pepper to taste just before serving.

Eggplant Purée
Kahrmus

STEP 1 Peel eggplant and cube in 1" squares to make 3 cups. Steam in colander over boiling water for 30 minutes.

STEP 2 Heat in wide saucepan:
  ¼ cup oil

Add into hot oil:
>   2 cloves garlic, finely diced
> $\frac{1}{2}$ teaspoon salt
> $\frac{1}{2}$ teaspoon black pepper
>   1 teaspoon sweet red pepper
>   the eggplant

Stir constantly for 10 minutes or until vegetable becomes a purée.

SERVE Hot, immediately.

Potato Stew
L'Petata Btskulya

Preheat in casserole:
>   1 cup oil

Add quickly, one by one to hot oil:
>   1 tablespoon sweet red pepper
>   1 cup water
>   1 tablespoon salt
>   1 tablespoon ground cumin seed
> $\frac{1}{2}$ cup parsley, chopped fine
>   1 head garlic, peeled, chopped fine
>   2 lbs potatoes, peeled and quartered
>   2 additional cups water
>   1 lemon rind (yellow part only) finely diced

Cook over a steady fire until potatoes are done.

Bean Pot (1)
Lubia

STEP 1 Add together in pot:
>   1 lb beans (navy, kidney, white beans)
>   1 onion, whole
>   1 head garlic (unpeeled)
>   1 quart water

Cover and cook over high fire until done; drain off *half* the remaining liquid.

STEP 2 Put in saucepan:
>   1 head garlic, peeled and minced

¼ cup parsley, minced
1 teaspoon hot red peppers
1 tablespoon sweet red pepper
2 laurel leaves
2 tablespoons salt
1 cup oil

Bring above ingredients to a boil; then add:

2 cups tomatoes, crushed
1 teaspoon ground cumin seed
1 cup water

STEP 3 When Step 2 again boils, add it to the beans. Return to fire until all again boils. It is then ready to serve.

Bean Pot (2)

Lubia
(Serves 4)

STEP 1 Put in deep pot:

1 lb dry white beans (which have soaked several hours in water)
1 onion, whole
1 head of garlic, peeled
1½ quarts cold water

Cover over medium fire until beans are tender (approx. 1½ hrs).

STEP 2 When beans are almost cooked, warm up in frying pan:

1 cup oil

Add to hot (not boiling) oil:

1 large onion, diced fine
1 cup parsley, chopped fine
1 teaspoon black pepper
2 tablespoons salt
¼ teaspoon saffron
½ cup water

When mixture boils, add it to the beans in their water. Mix well and continue cooking for 15 minutes. Then drain off excess water.

Note If beans are prepared some time before eating do not take the next step until ready to serve dish, and first reheat beans.

STEP 3 Break into hot beans:

    3 raw eggs

Mix eggs well into beans; they will cook almost instantly in the heat already generated.

SERVE Immediately.

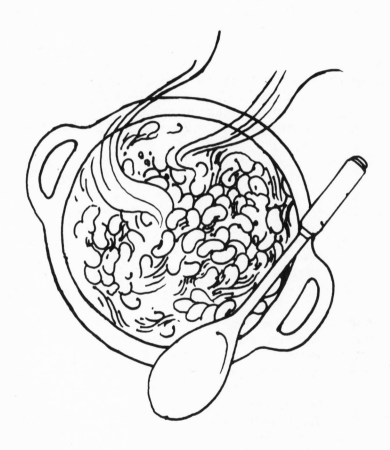

BREADS AND PASTRIES

Moroccan Tea Cakes
Braewats

STEP 1 Blanch, remove skins, and toast almonds very lightly. Add to the almonds enough sugar to make them very sweet, and grind this mixture together.

STEP 2 Roll out and cut ordinary pastry dough in rectangular leaves, about 6″ × 4″. Grease each leaf with butter or olive oil. Spread each thinly with almond-sugar mixture. Fold over a tiny bit of the dough at each end, then roll up, jelly-roll style.

STEP 3 Fry pastry in deep oil until a light brown. Then lay each braewat in boiling honey and leave for 5–10 minutes.

SERVE Cold, with tea, or as a dessert.

Variation Braewats are also made with almonds which have been blanched and peeled, but not toasted.

Date and Almond Cookies
T'Smahr bi Looz Mitabukeen

STEP 1 Blend well together:
  ¼ cup butter (or margarine)
  ½ cup honey
Add into the above, and beat well:
  1 egg
  1 tablespoon lemon juice
Then add, mixing well:
  1 cup fine flour
  ½ teaspoon salt
  ¼ teaspoon baking soda
  ⅛ teaspoon cream of tartar
  1 cup dates, cut up fine
  1 cup almonds (raw or slightly toasted), blanched and ground up or chopped fine

STEP 2 Make drop cookies on greased baking sheet. Bake in hot oven for under 10 minutes.

Egg Cookies
T'Smahr

STEP 1 Stir well together:
4 whole eggs
6 egg yolks
Add:
$\frac{1}{8}$ teaspoon salt
$\frac{1}{8}$ teaspoon baking soda
$\frac{1}{8}$ teaspoon cream of tartar
3 cups sugar
sufficient fine flour to bring to drop-cookie consistency.
Dough will be sticky

STEP 2 Make drop cookies on greased baking sheet. Bake in hot oven for about 10 minutes. Dust lightly with flour on removing from oven.

Bread
L'Hobz

Moroccan bread is rather heavy, but tasty and nutritious; it is a round disk made from flour which is not highly refined. People who 'know' this bread can walk through the market where, early in the morning or late in the afternoon, the unwrapped warm loaves are piled high at open-air booths and tell by looking at them – or pinching them – which is the loaf they want.

Since many different families and many different bakers share the use of communal ovens, each family or baker stamps the top of its loaves with some identifying mark.

Arabs bake bread on flat, airy surfaces (not in tins) in a great, cavernous community oven which has been heated by wood or charcoal – and the fire itself removed. With the use of a kind of long-handled shovel, the loaves are introduced into the oven, where the heat circulates freely around them. Once done on one side, they are flipped over.

This is the standard bread recipe:

STEP 1 Mix together:

3 cups lukewarm water

2 teaspoons salt

½ cup yeast (or 2 teaspoonsful of leavening in powder form)

To the above add:

6½ cups coarse flour

STEP 2 Knead well until it reaches bread dough consistency. Divide into portions, moulding each loaf into a 1-inch high round disk about 8 inches in diameter. This recipe will provide about 3 of the flattish loaves. Place loaves on a floured board, cover with a cloth and leave for 2 hours to raise, then bake.

Breakfast Doughnuts
Sfinjes

Pavement-stands make these doughnut-shaped pastries, and early morning customers may be seen carrying them home, 6 or 8 tied in a loop by a long blade of grass or palmetto blade. They go well with coffee.

STEP 1 Knead together into a stiff dough for ½ hour:

1 lb flour

1 oz leavening

warm water

Knead until the dough bubbles, then add more warm water, kneading well until the dough is reduced to a thick paste. It should still be thick enough to be able to be pulled, and stringy. It is then left to ferment for 20–30 minutes, when bubbles should rise freely.

STEP 2 Tear away a small portion of dough; pierce the centre and pull dough out into a ring. Repeat. Drop these in boiling oil, turn over when browned on one side.

SERVE Dredged in sugar or honey.

Gazelles' Horns
Kabulzel

Visitors to southern Morocco will be able to buy Gazelles' Horns –

one of the best of Moroccan pastries – at pavement stands in Casablanca, Rabat, Marrakech and Fez. The semi-sweet almond-filled patty, best produced in Marrakech and Fez kitchens, takes its name from its curved crescent shape, rather than from any association with the vanishing species.

The recipe given here makes ten good-sized tarts. The ingredients may be doubled for more, and since preparation takes time, it may seem worthwhile to make a fair-sized batch.

STEP 1 The pastry: make pastry dough and form into balls of a size which easily fit into the palm of the hand. Roll out to leaves 6″ in diameter, medium-thin thickness. I suggest using the conventional pastry dough which is richer, but for the record, the following is the recipe for making Arabic pastry dough.

Add together:

3½ cups flour
1 cup orange blossom water (or water)

Knead well, then shape into balls, working with a little melted butter. Then roll out.

STEP 2 The filling: blend well together in a paste:

2 cups raw almonds, blanched, peeled and ground
1 tablespoon cinnamon
1 tablespoon orange blossom water (or water)
½ cup sugar

STEP 3 On the lower half of each pastry circle, place in a crescent shape, 1 large tablespoon full of almond filling. Fold the other half of the pastry leaf over it and pinch shut. Pinch off excess dough in the middle. Bake 10–15 minutes in a hot oven on a lightly floured metal baking sheet; they should not be too well baked. Gazelles' Horns keep well if stored in an airtight tin.

Variation In Fez the pastries are only very slightly baked, so that the dough appears under-done. They are often then given this next extra treatment.

Boil together a thin mixture of orange blossom water (or water) and icing sugar until it is slightly sticky. Allow syrup to cool off until it is only warm. The *kabulzel* are dipped in this, then rolled in powdered sugar and left overnight. In the morning before use (they are often eaten for breakfast), the loose sugar is brushed off.

Fackasch

(A small, flat disk of semi-sweet bread – for tea and weddings.)

STEP 1 Mix together:

2 teaspoons salt

½ cup yeast (or 2 teaspoonsful leavening in powder form)

1 teaspoon poppy seed

2 tablespoons aniseed

½ teaspoon caraway seed

2 tablespoons sugar

After blending above, add:

4 cups fine flour

sufficient lukewarm water to bring to bread dough consistency when mixed

STEP 2 After kneading into bread dough consistency, make balls, using a handful of dough for each, and flatten down. Allow to rise an hour on a floured board, and covered with a cloth. Bake in medium oven.

TARTS, NOODLES, RICE

Egg and Cheese Tart
Imjibinah
(For 6)

STEP 1 Make pastry dough. Roll out medium-thin to make 6 oblong leaves.

STEP 2 Blend thoroughly by hand:
2 tablespoons parsley, minced
2 tablespoons onion, minced
6 hardboiled eggs, crushed
1 cup mild fresh cheese, cubed coarsely
1 teaspoon salt
1 tablespoon cinnamon

STEP 3 Place $\frac{1}{6}$ of egg-cheese mixture on each leaf of pastry; fold over and pinch shut.

STEP 4 Fry tarts, one or two at a time in:
$\frac{1}{4}$ cup preheated oil (or butter)
or bake in preheated oven with a dab of butter on each.

Variations This tart is surprisingly good, sweetened in the Moroccan way. After baking or frying tarts, dip for a few minutes in a boiling mixture of:
1 cup sugar
1 tablespoon cinnamon
$\frac{1}{2}$ cup water

SERVE Hot, or warm, with or without sugar sprinkled on top.

A Moroccan Empanada
Mrroozeea
(Serves 6)

STEP 1 Put in deep pot:
6 cups cold water
2 tablespoons parsley, minced

　　　　1 teaspoon butter
　　　　½ teaspoon saffron
　　　　1 tablespoon salt
Bring above to boil, then add:
　　　　2 cups rice
When rice is *nearly* cooked, remove from fire, add cold water, then drain. When rice is well drained and nearly dry, mix into it:
　　　　1 tablespoon cinnamon
　　　　½ cup sugar (optional)
STEP 2 Slightly heat in frying pan:
　　　　¼ cup olive oil (or butter)
Add to heated oil:
　　　　3 tablespoons onion, minced
　　　　2 tablespoons parsley, minced
　　　　½ teaspoon paprika
　　　　1 teaspoon black pepper
　　　　1 teaspoon salt
Fry and stir well for a few minutes until onion is golden. Then add:
　　　　1 lb finely ground meat (beef or veal)
Mix and fry until meat is done; it should be loose and fine.
STEP 3 Have pastry dough ready, and roll out in medium-thin circles about 5″ in diameter.
　　　　Place 1 heaped tablespoonful of rice, and 1 heaped tablespoon fried ground meat on one-half of each pastry circle. Put a dot of butter atop each mound; fold over the other half of pastry, and pinch shut.
STEP 4 Bake in oven – or fry in the Moroccan way in hot oil.
SERVE Hot; reheat in oven if necessary.

A Judge's Turban
Ruzitt L'Kadi or Moroccan Noodles

STEP 1 Work 7 cups of flour and a little water into bread dough consistency using standard procedure. Knead well.

STEP 2 Dip the right hand into a cup of oil (the oil is important). Pull off a half handful of dough from the mass and begin working it into a fine strand. Wrap the growing strand around the left hand. Oil the right hand frequently and continue wrapping the lengthening strand until the left hand is fairly well wrapped around with loops.

Remove the coil, depositing it in its same 'turban' form on an oiled, floured baking sheet, and press it down very firmly with the palm of the hand.

Repeat the process of making 'judge's turbans' until the dough is used up.

STEP 3 In the Moroccan method, the 'turbans' are baked directly over the fire. When done on the bottom, they are turned over. A turban is finished when it turns the colour of light, golden oak.

STEP 4 Once turbans are baked and cooled, again wet the hand with oil, and taking each turban, shake it out. Each will separate into a whole loose coil.

SERVE Buttered and drenched in honey for tea *or* in chicken broth *or* with a little salt and butter in warm milk.

Spaghetti
Lifdowish
(Serves 6)

Put in deep pot on fire:
    6 cups water
    6 tablespoons butter
    $\frac{1}{2}$ cup onion, diced fine
    3 tablespoons parsley, minced
    $\frac{1}{2}$ teaspoon black pepper
    $\frac{1}{4}$ teaspoon saffron
    3 dessertspoons salt
When water boils, add:
    1 lb fine spaghetti
When spaghetti is cooked, drain off liquid, and turn out onto serving platter. Pour over spaghetti:
    1 cup honey
Sprinkle with:
    1 tablespoon cinnamon

FRUIT DESSERTS

Apple, Banana, Almond Dessert
Tfah, Banana, Laouz

STEP 1 Prepare and add together:
6 medium-size apples (preferably tart), peeled, cored, and sliced medium-fine
1 cup blanched, lightly toasted almonds, ground up
1 tablespoon cinnamon

STEP 2 Melt in saucepan:
$\frac{1}{2}$ cup butter

STEP 3 Add apple-almond mixture (Step 1) to melted butter in saucepan.

Then, over a high fire, one at a time, and mixing each in, add:
1 lemon rind, cut in very fine strips
(use only the fine thin yellow part of rind)
$\frac{1}{2}$ cup water
1 cup sugar
juice of one lemon
4 bananas, sliced

Mix frequently, cooking until sugar has dissolved and mixture is almost dry. Then add:
$\frac{1}{4}$ cup orange blossom water (substitute water if this is not available)

Continue cooking until mixture is quite dry. Apples should be tender, but not mushy.

SERVE Cool.

Apple Dessert
Tfah
(For 6)

STEP 1 Prepare and set aside:
8 apples, preferably tart, peeled, cored and sliced fine

the rind of 3 fresh lemons, cut into very fine strips (use only the yellow part of rind)

STEP 2 Put in saucepan over high fire:

2 cups granulated sugar
2 tablespoons cinnamon
2 cups water

When mixture boils, add:

apple and lemon rind from Step 1
½ cup lemon juice
½ cup orange blossom water (or plain water)

Continue cooking, stirring, until mixture is nearly dry.

SERVE Cooled, as dessert.

Note: If orange blossom water is not available, but orange blossoms are, wash the *petals only* of a bunch of the blossom – do *not* use the centre part of the flower – add the petals to ½ cup water and use in recipe.

Cinnamon Orange
Litcheen Bl Karfah Usukar

Allow one or more meaty, eating oranges for each serving. Peel and slice oranges in crosswise disks. Over each portion on serving plate, sprinkle:

½ teaspoon cinnamon
1 tablespoon sugar
orange blossom water, if available

Pomegranate
Rrumen Bjbn

Use one pomegranate for each serving portion. Remove the fruit from the shell and pulp. To each portion, add:

1 tablespoon mild cheese, grated
2 teaspoons honey

Date Loaf
Halua Ditzmar

Here is a natural sweet, a splendid fruit and nut combination, which originated in Algeria.

Blend together:

　　1 lb dates, stoned
　　1 lb figs, peeled and pounded
　　½ lb walnuts and pecans, chopped up coarsely
　　a little aniseed
　　2 tablespoons honey

After all ingredients are well blended, pack them into a solid loaf (an old cake tin will do). The loaf may be kept for some time and sliced as wanted.

Candied Oranges
Majoon di Litcheen

This is a Moroccan Jewish preparation from the town of Mogador. The oranges must be large, firm and meaty with thick skins.

STEP 1　Soak 1 dozen oranges 1½ hours in water. Drain. Scrape off the fine orange-coloured part of the rind. This should leave only the white pulp showing.

STEP 2　Wash oranges in two or three changes of salted water to remove any bitterness from the rind. Then drop them in boiling water and leave for a few minutes. Oranges should be heated right through, but do not allow them to get soft.

STEP 3　Drain and chill (in refrigerator). Cube oranges, slicing three or four times crosswise, then lengthwise.

STEP 4　Caramelize a lb of sugar in a frying pan. When sugar is caramelized, add oranges in over the fire, and mix well until the sugar penetrates oranges and gives them a golden colour. The sugar may even burn a little. Oranges should be very sweet, and after a few minutes the mess will be sticky rather than liquid. Remove from fire and cool. These may be kept over a long period of time in an airtight jar.

Note: The same method may be applied to lemon *peel* only, using thick lemon peels, and some lemon juice in the sugar.

PICKLES

Pickled Pilchard
Shtoon Fufarran

This is one of the best aperitif snacks I have ever tasted. Although it is also a Spanish dish, it is known throughout Northern Morocco, where fish abound, and the truth of its origin has been lost in the shuffle of time. Moroccans prepare and store it against rainy days when no one cares to go out and fishing is poor.

This recipe will pickle two or more pounds of fresh, tiny sardines, small herring, smelt, anchovies, or any other related small fish. It is an exciting dish. For big cocktail parties, double the recipe.

STEP 1 Wash fish quickly and lightly in cool salted water. Clean by snapping off heads between thumb and forefinger, and pulling towards yourself; the entrails come away easily at the same time.

STEP 2 Pour boiling hot salted water over the fish. Let stand in water for two minutes, during which time they split open. Drain off water and lift the vertebrae out of fish. The two halves of each thus separate in two tiny fillets.

STEP 3 Mix together the following and pound into a paste in the mortar:
1 head of garlic, peeled
½ cup parsley, minced
1 teaspoon hot red peppers
1 tablespoon ground cumin seed

STEP 4 In a deep dish large enough to easily accommodate fish, add, one at a time, and mixing in each ingredient:
spice paste (Step 3)
1 cup lemon juice (or light vinegar)
⅓ cup oil
2 tablespoons salt
¼ cup water
Mix well. Lay fish in this, and cover.

SERVE Cool, with cocktails or as appetizer. Kept cool and covered, it can be stored for a week.

Preserved Lemons (or Limes)
Hamid Msyiar

Lemons pickled in the manner of Moroccans from the city of Mequinez, heighten food flavours, and give just the right tart complement as garnish for roasts and stews. Those who will take the few minutes necessary to prepare them will be able to use them often in preparing dishes given here.

First, have handy and scalded, one or more wide-mouthed glass jars. Now, prepare a dozen or more firm, ripe lemons or limes at one time.

With a knife, slash the sides of each fruit lengthwise from top to bottom, making three or four gashes in each lemon or lime; but *do not* cut it apart. Stuff the gashes *generously* with salt. Don't be afraid of using too much.

Place the lemons in the jar, filling it to about three-quarters full; all but cover fruit with cold water, leaving some air at the top. Screw the lid on tight.

Leave to set ten days in a medium-warm place. After about that time, mould forms in the jar; remove this, clean the jar and change the water. Add some salt and re-seal. (This cleaning should be done only once.)

The pickled lemon is ready for use in about three weeks from the time of original preparation. The rind will be softened and tartly sweet.

SERVE   Sliced or diced (including rind) as garnish for meat, fish and fowl. Covered, they will keep two months or more.

Green Cocktail Olives
Zaytoon

Here is a recipe for preparing your own olives, with a special tang. This recipe is adequate to 10 lbs of olives.

Select perfect, unblemished raw olives. They may be green, white, yellow, reddish-brown or black.

STEP 1   Slash each olive two or three times with a knife, without cutting right through it. It is not necessary to remove the stones.

STEP 2 Place olives in a deep container – preferably a wooden barrel or deep clay pot. Add in and mix with olives:
3 lbs salt (not iodized)
5 fresh lemons, with rind, cubed small

STEP 3 Put a heavy weight on the top of the olives. Leave a week, then check. If the salt is all gone, add more. Pickling will take from three to four weeks, or until the bitterness has left them. When they can be eaten without having the mouth pucker, they are ready. Leave olives in the salt brine until wanted.

STEP 4 As olives are wanted for the table, take the desired amount out of the brine and dress them with a sauce of:
a generous amount of lemon juice
finely chopped hot red pepper (optional)

Allow to marinate in lemon juice a few hours before serving. (If all are to be used at once, add 3 cups lemon juice. This procedure may also be followed and the olives stored in airtight jars.)

Preserved Lemon Rind
H'Lemoon Kesharah

Don't throw away lemon rinds after squeezing the juice from them. With almost no preparation they make an interesting garnish for meat, fish and fowl.

Fill the rinds with salt and store in a sealed jar or well-covered clay pot in a dry place. They will turn a leatherish colour and be ready for use in about 4 to 6 weeks.

When wanted for the table; soak rind in a bowl of water for three hours to remove excess salt. Change water twice during the three hours.

BEVERAGES

Contrary to general opinion, Coca-Cola is not the Moroccans' national drink, although it may come close to it, and can be found in the most unlikely places. Denied alcoholic beverages by their religion, water being at certain times and places undrinkable, people quench their thirst by perking up other beverages.

Mint Tea
Etzay

Mint tea is the most popular drink and is described on page 57. It is made simply with a base of green China tea and the addition of fresh mint leaves, plus orange blossom petals or rose petals when in season.

Coffee
Kah-wa

When Moroccans drink coffee, it is very strong and very sweet like the Turkish variety.

For 1 glassful of coffee, 1 teaspoonful of coffee beans is first toasted very dark in a ladle over the fire. These are then pounded to a powder. A tiny, long-handled lidless copper pot is filled with water and held over the charcoal fire in a tiny oven until the water boils. The coffee powder is then added to the water, and the pot returned to the fire. When it has boiled for a minute, a teaspoonful of cinnamon is added, and the coffee brought to a boil. Removed from the heat it is set aside for a minute to let the sediment settle. The brew is served, very hot and very sweet, in a thin glass to which much sugar is added.

Orange Juice
Litcheen Awasahr

Some of the best oranges in the world are grown in Morocco, and in December, their season, are practically given away. Moroccans vary the taste with the addition of:

$\frac{1}{2}$ teaspoon cinnamon
$\frac{1}{2}$ teaspoon sugar
1 tablespoon orange blossom water (if available)

Samit

The Kentucky mountaineers and the Irish are not the only country folk to have discovered the secret of making potables. In Chauen, a charming mountain city some forty miles from Tangier, where streams are fed the year round by melting snow you will find samit sold in stone jugs in the shops. The town was founded 500 years ago by Moors expelled from Granada. This is how the samit is made:

Mixed grapes are pounded up and boiled to half their original bulk. This takes about twelve hours. The boiled grapes are then added to an equal quantity of unboiled fresh grapes, and left a month to ferment. The liquor is then skimmed and bottled. For a thicker, sweeter variety, much sugar is added in the boiling process.

MISCELLANEOUS

Gruel for Children
Shorbah Ndreree
(For 2 small children)

STEP 1 Toast lightly in oven or dry pan atop stove:
$\frac{1}{4}$ cup chick-peas (which have soaked overnight in water) *or*
$\frac{1}{4}$ cup almonds, blanched
Grind chick-peas up fine and mix them with:
$\frac{1}{4}$ teaspoon cinnamon
STEP 2 Heat in small saucepan:
1 cup milk
When skim forms on milk, add one by one over the fire, stirring each in:
the chick-pea meal
1 medium-sized potato, mashed
1 heaped tablespoon sugar
Stir constantly until mixture boils, then add:
1 teaspoon butter
a pinch of salt
Continue cooking, and stirring, until mixture thickens slightly.
SERVE Lukewarm.

Blanched and Toasted Almonds

Drop almonds in boiling water and leave on fire for 2 minutes; remove from fire but allow almonds to steep for a moment in the hot water. Then chill quickly in cold water. Drain, blot dry and rub off the skins.

Heat 2 or 3 tablespoons olive oil (or butter) in a frying pan. Drop almonds, *very* lightly sprinkled with a tiny pinch of salt, into the hot oil. Stir and turn over constantly until they reach a light golden shade. Remove from oil immediately; (the heat retained in almonds continues to brown them further even after they have been removed from heat). Blot dry and leave to cool.

If almonds are to be salted, do not salt until nearly dried and crisp – or if to be eaten alone, salt just before eating. Those used in recipes in this book are not to be salted after toasting.

Note on Garnish

Many Moroccan tables always bear a dish of crushed cumin seed mixed with salt, for seasoning meats, etc. at table. Try seasoning hard-boiled eggs this way instead of with salt alone.

Madjoon

Like other Moroccan favourites, madjoon is made in a variety of ways, some of which have a chocolatey flavour. It is cut in squares like fudge and many Westerners who have tried it know it as fudge or hashish fudge. Some kinds are almost entirely a compound of spices, and can be bought in hunks or large heavy balls in shops of interior towns, where it is weighed out by the kilo just as sugar is. Some insist the best recipes for it contain ground porcupine.

Madjoon, is Old Morocco's party mixer, blues chaser, relaxer and general elixir. Although this is a law-breaking recipe in most places, I give it as a matter of interest because it is famous in Tangier.

STEP I Take as many stalks of the female hemp plant (*Cannabis Indica*) as can be grasped in a normal hand. Remove carefully and discard all the long thin yellow leaves. This will leave only the short green leaves around the seeds on the stalk. Remove the small green leaves and place them on a metal tray. (Throw the stalk away.) Dry leaves well in the sun or over a gentle heat until they are brittle. Then rub them between your hands, removing the seeds, which are discarded. Rub the crushed leaves through a sieve. (An ordinary tea strainer will do.) It should become powdery.

STEP 2 Wash, then dry well over heat:
  ½ breakfast cup sesame seed
Rub between the hands, removing any husk from:
  2 good handfuls caraway seed

Blend the sesame and caraway seeds with:
    1 tablespoon honey
Heat all over fire for 5 minutes, stirring well.

STEP 3 Next, rub between hands, removing stalk from:
    a good handful of aniseed

STEP 4 Crush in a mortar and pass through a sieve:
    20 cloves
    6 nutmegs
    enough ginger root to make a handful when passed through
      sieve
    1 handful powdered cinnamon

STEP 5 Shell and crush:
    ½ lb walnuts

STEP 6 Wash and dry in a pan over a low heat with a sprinkling
    of the crushed nuts:
    1 scant lb seedless raisins

STEP 7 Chop up:
    6 large dates, seeded

STEP 8 Mix well together all the preceding ingredients except
    the hemp, working with the hands as if making dough.
Work in:
    7 tablespoons honey
When well blended, spread mixture out over a working surface
such as a bread board. Now put 2 tablespoons of the powdered
hemp in a very fine cloth or exceptionally fine strainer. Dust this
over the blended ingredients. Next, spread over surface:
    2 tablespoons of honey.
Continue this process of dusting 2 tablespoons of hemp alternately
with 2 tablespoons honey, until hemp is used up. Then leave
mass to set while hemp absorbs the honey for ½ hour or until honey
reaches a tough consistency.

STEP 9 Cook madjoon over a brisk fire, stirring constantly, for
    20–30 minutes, or until mixture is nearly dry. When
    finished it should be of the consistency of stiff jam.

SERVE Cool, eaten with a teaspoon. The older it is, the better.
    It should be stored in a glass or plastic jar with lid on.
    Servings should be limited to two teaspoons per person.
Antidote: occasionally, the mixture may prove too strong for

the novice in which case the effects may be annulled by drinking hot lemonade made of:

> 1 cup boiling water
> juice of a lemon
> a few grains of salt
> 2 teaspoons sugar

Note Complete evaporation of moisture in basic ingredient is necessary in order that madjoon can be kept longer than a month. Thus prepared, we are told, it can be kept for as long as five years.

The Wedding Breakfast
Sefh'a
(A Dish for Two)

According to tradition, the wedding breakfast following the first night of Moslem marriage consists of a highly nourishing rice dish called sefh'a. We suggest it for any who have had a heavy night, and although the plate is clearly specified for two, the results allow for a third.

STEP 1 Bring to a boil:

> 1 quart milk
> 1 pint water

When liquid boils, throw in:

> 2 cups rice

When rice is cooked, chill and separate the grains, ('frighten it' according to my Moroccan respondent), by pouring in:

> 2 cups cold water

Drain off the liquid.

STEP 2 Melt in saucepan:

> 7 tablespoons butter

Add rice to butter, stirring. Return to fire and add, stirring:

> 5 tablespoons honey (or sugar)

Remove from fire when well blended, or when sugar, in case it is used, is melted.

SERVE Hot, garnished with sugar and cinnamon.

A COOK IN
THE KASBAH

The youngster was small for his seven years, but his big black eyes observed everything, missed nothing. Like many Moroccan youngsters he spent his time hanging about the sunny streets or listening to the talk of men.

His father had sent him to school when he was six, to a tiny room where twenty boys simultaneously memorized the Koran. Few studied the same text at the same time. The cacophony of high sing-song voices grated in Mohammed's ears, and he dreamed. Before a year was out he left school forever.

Sometimes he ran errands for a housewife, with excursions into the *souks* with their spice stalls and mounds of foods. He loved the colours – the reds of ripe tomatoes, and raw meats, the rich greens of parsley, the orange flame of peppers, the gold of lemons and oranges and carrots. Such errands earned him a few pennies, and to make sure all turned out as it should, he often hung about the kitchen later to sample whatever dish was being prepared.

Kitchens held a special attraction for him. The soft warming glow from the charcoal cooking pots drew him to their comfort on a cold day, and the savoury fragrance of stews blended with fresh spices were perfume to a boy who often went hungry.

One breathless summer day he lingered near a shop doorway. Inside, a man was buying sacks of dates, raisins, almonds.

'Hey, you!' he called the boy. 'Help me get these to the train!'

With some effort, the youngster heaved a sack as large as himself onto his shoulder, and they made their way to the station some blocks away.

'Do you have any family?' the man asked.

'*La, ualoo,*' (no, none) he lied.

'Nobody?'

'Nobody.'

Homeless youngsters are not uncommon in Middle-Eastern countries, and adoption of them is an informal affair. They gain a home in exchange for their help in house, workshop or farm, becoming one of the family and often remaining so even after marriage, until old age and death. There is much to be said for this social arrangement, even though it is occasionally abused, and an old Magrebi proverb says that a parent may love his child so dearly that he will abandon him (thus allowing him a better destiny).

'Do you want to come and work with me? I'll make you my son,' said the stranger.

'All right,' replied Mohammed, and he climbed with the man onto the black monster of a train for the first time in his life.

By the time they arrived in Sidil Yemani, a tiny Foreign Legion outpost tucked some twenty miles away in the hills, he had learned, much to his delight, that this new father was a pastry cook.

The days of work began, and the boy ran and fetched and carried for the baker, Abslem. Doughs must be pulled and punched and kneaded into fluffiness. With a long-handled flat shovel he would lift the pastries and bread into the gaping cavern of the oven. It was big enough for one his size to walk about in when cooled, and if its hot blasts left him near fainting in July, they were a blessing in winter. As the bakery was attached to Abslem's home, he would curl up on the floor close to it at night to sleep. One day they would bake and the next day, as dawn broke over the African hills, they would be on their way, carrying the cakes and sweetmeats to the shop in town to sell. There they stayed until nightfall, selling their wares and chatting with villagers. Home and family seemed far away, and even when occasionally he yearned to see his mother, there was old Mrs Abslem to mother and scold him. And from her he learned to cook the *tazjeens* of mutton in oil, made savoury with cardamon and cumin seed and onions. From the baker he learned to make the sweets called *braewats*.

One day the baker told him to remain at home to prepare an extra supply of sweets for a Saint's feast. The boy worked all day long, and when Abslem failed to return by midnight, he and the baker's wife decided their lord and master was spending the night in town. They shot the great bolt on the outside door and slept.

At five in the morning a loud knocking aroused Mohammed. Shivering, he opened the door to a neighbour who shuddered and groaned, beside himself with agitation. When finally the man could speak he told the story of Abslem's assassination. The baker had been waylaid and killed as he walked home, and his money stolen. Then, so that the last scene of his life might not remain permanently recorded to witness against them, his murderers had removed his eyes.

The obsequies over, Mohammed remained, having been a part of the family for a year or more. The oven was still there; he knew the business. The baker's widow advanced him money for flour and sugar, honey and almonds, so, at the age of nine he became a baker, making the candies and pastries he had learned to make in his apprenticeship, and remembering always to add lots of colour.

Not content to sit and wait for customers, Mohammed carried his wares to the country markets and mountain hamlets, seated high on a mule between the two full panniers. One village, Hadd L'Arbia, had its big market day on Sundays, another, L'Tineen Yemani, on Mondays. On Tuesdays the circuit of itinerant vendors took them to Keltza Sjbel Habib, where the *socco* called 'The Doves' is so named for its beautiful women.

On Fridays, the young merchant returned home to Sidil Yemani to spend the day and the night mixing and baking new batches of pastries.

To the north, he heard tell, there was a city, a mecca for foreigners and Moroccans alike: a city of Western lights and Western ways where strange European inventions filled the shops. Now he had money of his own, and a mule, so he could indulge his adventurous nature. Alone he set out on the forty-mile journey through the hills to Tangier on the sea.

He had not yet reached the age of fourteen when a boy becomes a man and shaves his head to don a turban. Like other boys of the Jibála hill Berber tribes, he wore part of his head shaven, with the remaining hair in a *kurn* (a queue pulled tight to the back and side of his head). In the tradition of his region, a large metal loop hung from his pierced right ear. And under the brown wool country *djellabah* was the traditional, high-buttoned Arab suit of clothing.

Thus it was that late one afternoon he rode along the sandstrip bordering the bay at Tangier, where for the first time, he saw people bathing in the sea. He urged his mule up the hill to the *souks* of the Big Market, which teemed with people, shouting, and selling all manner of goods, from herbs and foods to cooking pots and flowers and cloth.

As the picturesque young outlander rode into a *fondak*, a *Nazrenie* (Christian) walked towards him. The man carried a small black box which he pointed towards the mountain boy. 'Click!' it went; then, smiling, the man handed Mohammed five *pesetas*. For a moment Mohammed had been frightened, but now he was pleased. Here one got money for nothing. He had never seen or heard of a camera before.

Life centred about the *socco* with its teeming movement and the daily comings and goings of country people with their laden animals. A constant hubbub of voices rose in selling and bargaining and buying. Straw-hatted country women sat in rows with their baskets of eggs, calling out to passers-by. Behind them, the clutter of vegetables and fruits and flowers vied in brilliant reds and yellows with the wares of cloth-sellers across the way. There were fragrant bread stalls and fish fresh from the sea and spices . . . all the ingredients necessary for the *tadjeen* one would cook over a charcoal pot inside the *fondak*. From morning till night, when kerosene torches lighted the area, the *socco* was a theatre in constant motion and a source of information, accurate and otherwise.

The *Nazrenie* women came to buy too, some being followed by a man in uniform who carried their market baskets. Often the boy went up to their part of town to watch these strangers and their life. He was fascinated by these 'Europeans', the Dutch, the English, the Americans, the French, the Germans and the Scandinavians, with their quick light speech, their odd and interesting European dress and their fine cars. Though they alarmed him at first, curiosity overcame fear, and he would follow close behind them on the pavements to listen and observe.

By the end of the first week young Mohammed had cut off his queue, sold his mule, and traded his native clothes for a second-hand European suit.

By the end of the second week he had made the acquaintance of a band of *trappelistas* – smugglers – who made the 120-mile daily round train trip between Tangier and Alczar-el-Kebir. From that citadel they brought cheap goods to sell in the city: cloth, jewellery, soap, sugar, pepper, coffee and green tea. A contrabandist must be clever to escape customs inspection, and often the loot is hidden among the voluminous folds of the women's *haiks*. Inspectors often close one eye, for smuggling is one way

poor people have of making a living. Smuggling is, after all, a
business. By the end of his third week in Tangier, Mohammed
had entered the business.

The day was often a long one and he would neglect to eat until
he returned to the city. Then his greatest pleasure lay in preparing
his meal. Often it was the liver, heart and kidney from a freshly
slaughtered lamb, seasoned with hot red pepper, parsley, salt and
cumin seed, then spitted on wire skewers and barbecued over
glowing red charcoal. Here, too, he discovered the goodness of
seafoods, and in experimenting with these, learned to combine
shrimp with eggs in an omelette, and to dress the huge mussels and
tiny clams with vinegar, oil and hot spices. Sometimes while the
tadjeens simmered in the cooking pots, sending up mouth-watering
perfumes, he amused himself by drawing on wrapping paper.

One afternoon he sat on the station platform awaiting the train
when a face which was vaguely familiar appeared before him.

'*Ash ka tsaamel hna?*' ('What are you doing here?') the man
asked him in Magrebi.

'Waiting for the train.'

'What's your name?'

'Ismee Mohammed. And you?'

'My name is Robert. *Ana Merekanee.*' ('I am an American.')

The man sat down on the platform beside him, and chatted
leisurely, telling of the photo he had taken of a young mountain
boy with his long queue, astride a mule. They talked, too, about
cooking.

Perhaps Destiny looks after those of its children whose minds
are open on all sides. That afternoon Mohammed went with the
American to his home, where he was installed as cook.

Here he had a whole kitchen to himself in which to cook as he
pleased, and to experiment. First shopping carefully, he laboured
with devotion over his steaming casseroles. And if the preparations
were time-consuming, his reward lay in surprising his patrons with
foods the Americans had never before tasted, and in his delight at
the household's obvious enjoyment of Moroccan cuisine. Love and
respect for food and its treatment went into his work. To make it
attractive to the eye, he always blended enough saffron and sweet
red pepper to lend colour. One day he would carry to the table a
bowl of whole small chickens, golden with saffron and olive oil, and
garnished with green olives or sweetly tart preserved lemon; the

next day, a whole fish, even more beautiful than when it came from the sea, stuffed with garlic and drenched in butter and parsley.

One evening the *Merekanee* announced important guests for the next afternoon, among them a prince from the city of Fez.

'Shall we show him you are truly a chef? What do you suggest we give a prince for lunch?'

Cook for a prince! Surely this must be the apex of glory for a country boy. So excited was he that he barely slept that night and rose at 6.00 a.m. to be early in the market place, and then to spend the entire morning preparing the *diffa*.

First he gave them omelette with shrimp spiced lightly with cumin seed, parsley and garlic; then rich-meated swordfish steaks sautéed in butter and dressed in smooth red tomato sauce well seasoned with spices and lemon rind; then one of the best of all Moroccan dishes, chicken with eggs and almonds and spices. Lastly, there was a *couscous* topped by a dressing of sweetened onions, raisins and almonds.

The results so pleased the guest of honour that while the party sipped mint tea later, the cook was called in and presented. Where, asked the prince, was he from?

'I am from Alczar-el-Kebir, but I am Berber.'

'Ho! And are the Berbers more gifted than the Fezzi?' the prince joked. 'Where did you learn to cook?'

'I learned by myself – here and there.'

'Would you like to come to Fez and work for me in the palace?'

Surely this royal young man was joking, and the boy replied in a similar light vein, laughing: 'Don't let the *Merekanee* hear you say that or we'll *both* be in the street.'

The prince left his card, nevertheless, and said that his house was the boy's whenever he liked; and in token of his appreciation for the excellence of the food, he took off his fine wool French necktie and gave it to the cook before departing.

'Where did you get that *djellabah*?' I asked Mohammed one day. It was of finely spun silk in black and white stripes, and extremely handsome, if a bit worn.

'Fez,' he replied, simply. Then, after a moment's silence, he told me the story of his palace days.

While he cooked for the *Merekanee* the thought of visiting the prince's famous city became increasingly tempting. So one after-noon, after a few months, when his natural restlessness grew beyond containment, he clambered down out of the third-class coach at Fez.

Approaching the old driver of a horse-drawn carriage he asked him if he knew where to find the house of Prince Mulay A———?

'Heavens above,' replied the old one, openly amused by the ignorance of this outlander. 'You mean our Saint. Everybody knows where he lives. Get in!'

The way seemed long in the dark, and a growing anxiety as to whether the prince would even remember him caused him to doubt the wisdom of this trip. Finally they stopped beside high palace walls, the driver descended and clanged the great brass door-knocker. A door swung back, revealing a glimmer of light, and the porter called a message into the interior behind him. Much to Mohammed's relief, the prince himself appeared after some minutes.

'Welcome to my home,' the prince greeted him. 'Come in. I am happy to see you.'

They crossed a magnificently gardened patio where a fountain splashed in the dark. Mohammed was really here, a Guest of a Prince in a Palace! It was a Moroccan dream come true. Following supper and tea, he was shown to a room all to himself for the night.

Morning splashed bright inside the green gardens and white buildings. The architecture had been designed to help man's spirit to soar. The vaulted rooms were suffused with light entering through the honeycomb tracery of bays arching the entrances. Here were ceilings of finely wrought woods inlaid in floral patterns and colours. The intricate designs of the wall tiles provided more exquisite decoration. Rich rugs covered the floors between the sofas. Crystal and silver and brass artefacts stood or hung on all sides. This indeed was luxury; and the abundant service and excellent food completed the dream every young Arab holds of living the life of a Sultan.

The prince, in the tradition of the good host, accompanied his humble young friend to see the sights of Fez. Everywhere there was colour and beauty to fill the eye – so much new to assimilate, so much to be learned. Outside the clamour and colour of the *souks* there were the jasmined Bou Jlud and Dar Batha gardens in which to walk. And each time the prince was recognized, his subjects bowed low and kissed his hand. Mohammed bathed in the glow of reflected glory.

Several days of this honeyed existence flowed by. On the morning of the fourth day, the prince called his guest to him.

'Good morning,' he said quietly, with a twinkle in his eyes. 'I trust you have slept well.' Mohammed assured him he had.

'Now then, Mohammed,' continued his host, 'As you know, the length of a visit as prescribed by custom is three days. Off to the kitchen with you!'

And he went.

The kitchen was governed by Blossom, a large lumbering negress whose command was law. Five young negresses were her subjects, and along with them, Mohammed set to work. Under her watchful eye he learned even more about cooking: how to make the feather-light pastry for *bastela*; how to cook the carrots and peas and pimentos, which abound in this rich agricultural region, in with the meat stews; how to let the raisins steep in water for a long time before adding them to *couscous*.

Sometimes, when all was prepared and waiting the command to serve, time lagged. To while it away the girls turned to what for them is the most natural thing besides breathing – the making of rhythm and music. First one began idly to sing, accompanying herself by drumming her hands on a bench. Another joined her. A third, clapping hands, began a slow, barefoot shuffle, a loose-limbed motion in which she moved only the upper part of her body, then only the hips, which caught the rhythm and increased in tempo as yet another joined in, thundering on a copper kettle. The boy added to the harmony with the reed flute that most Moroccan youngsters know how to play. The music, African and rhythmic and melodic, caught them all up in its excitement. This alone was worth the visit to Fez he decided, and being in the kitchen was altogether a good thing.

Mohammed stayed on, learning more and more about cooking, until he felt the call of the 'big city' with its lights and cinema. African warmth spilled over in tears when he announced his departure. When on his last morning he left the palace, the prince accompanied him.

'Come along to the *souks*,' said the prince, 'I want to find a gift for you.'

Already the merchants were removing the board fronts from the square boxes of shops. Inside the colour-hung passages, sun-shafts slanted through the latticed thatch shelter to trace designs on the hard-packed clay thoroughfare. Laden donkeys moved doggedly about their business as drivers shouted, *'Balek, balek!'* ('make way') and even a prince moved aside to let them pass.

Hung around the shop doorways, red leather hassocks and yellow goatskin *baboushes* vied for attention with burnished brass bowls and candlestick holders and etched silver and copper trays. Glazed pottery in traditional Moroccan blues jostled tiles of Arabesque design and rich satin cloths shot with gold, and colourful basketry. Rugs hand-woven in the Atlas Mountains draped the walls in reds, blues and beiges to lend luxury and furnishing.

Each time an object caught the boy's eye, his host noticed and picking it up, handed it to him. A small rug found its way into the boy's arms, as did two *djellabahs*, leather slippers, shoes, two tea trays, a flute, a *ginbri*, a *burnous*, a wallet, an embossed leather book and more, so that a porter was hired to carry the overflow.

As they moved from stall to stall, no money changed hands. The prince business, the boy decided privately, must be a good thing, and he exclaimed: 'But – you don't pay!'

'Ha, for I have no purse,' replied the young man, laughing. The bowing merchants, pleased to have his patronage, never thought of payment.

'Remember,' the prince called after Mohammed as the train pulled out. 'When you get tired of wherever you are, you know where your home is.'

There are few people, of course, even in Morocco, whose cooking experience has ranged so widely as Mohammed's; but his story has always seemed to me to contain the many elements gathered together in the country's cuisine, just as it does those contained in its life, from the simplest rural level to the palace. I have told it here in the hope that for you, too, it will add charm to the recipes in this book.

Islamic Holidays

Eid-el-Seghir (or *Eid-el-Fetra*) 'The Little Feast' falls at the end of the month of Ramadan. At this time Moslems must forgive one another their misdeeds and give alms to the poor.

Eid-el-Kebir 'The Big Feast' commemorates Abraham's sacrifice and follows the end of Ramadan by about two months. The head of each family kills a sheep, and the well-to-do share with the poor.

Achoura, the tenth day of the Moslem year, commemorates Moses and falls one month after Eid-el-Kebir.

Moulud celebrates the Prophet's birthday.

These holidays do not fall on the same day every year, nor at exactly the same number of days after each other each year, since the Moslems use the lunar calendar. There are also holidays of national or political significance e.g., the Day of the Throne, the Day of Independence, etc.

Glossary

Ambariya Curtained box, mounted usually on camel or horse, in which bride is concealed, and carried from her parents' home to that of her groom.

Bab Door.
Baboushas Heelless slippers.
Barakaoufik Thank you; please.
Bismillah Grace, usually said before eating: 'In the name of God'.

Cadi Judge
Caid Tribal leader, often mayor of a small town.

Dahir Decree signed by Sultan.
Darbooka Shallow drum.
Diffa Banquet.
Djellabah Tailored street-length, hooded cloak, worn by men and women.

Gaita Horn which sounds like bagpipe.
Ginbri Two-stringed guitar-like instrument.

Hamman Public steam bath.
Haik Draped, white, sheet-like covering worn in public by women.
Haiti Wall hanging, used to face interior walls, usually bear design of keyhole arches, in beiges and browns.
Hand of Fatima Symbolic emblem in shape of hand, protects wearer.

Inshallah Exclamation meaning: 'If God wills', or 'May God be willing'.

Kif Indian hemp – local brand of hashish.

Le bas Greeting equivalent to 'How are you?'.
La The word for 'No'.

Minaret Tower of a mosque.
Muezzin (or *Muadhahim*) Caller to prayers.

Safi 'Enough'.

Sarawel Bloomer-type trousers, usually colourful or patterned, which reach to just below the knee, worn by both men and women. The women wear them under their dresses.

Tambour Open-end clay drum.

Tarboush Red felt fez-type head covering worn by men.

Index